D0906448

Cambridge Studies in French

THE LIMITS OF
NARRATIVE

Cambridge Studies in French

General editor: MALCOLM BOWIE

THE LIMITS OF NARRATIVE

ESSAYS ON BAUDELAIRE, FLAUBERT, RIMBAUD AND MALLARMÉ

NATHANIEL WING

*Department of French and Italian
Louisiana State University,
Baton Rouge*

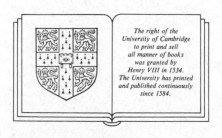

The right of the
University of Cambridge
to print and sell
all manner of books
was granted by
Henry VIII in 1534.
The University has printed
and published continuously
since 1584.

CAMBRIDGE UNIVERSITY PRESS

CAMBRIDGE

LONDON   NEW YORK   NEW ROCHELLE

MELBOURNE   SYDNEY

Published by the Press Syndicate of the University of Cambridge
The Pitt Building, Trumpington Street, Cambridge CB2 1RP
32 East 57th Street, New York, NY 10022, USA
10 Stamford Road, Oakleigh, Melbourne 3166, Australia

First published 1986

Printed in Great Britain at
the University Press, Cambridge

British Library cataloguing in publication data
Wing, Nathaniel
The limits of narrative: essays on Baudelaire, Flaubert, Rimbaud
and Mallarmé. – (Cambridge studies in French)
1. French literature – 19th century – History and criticism
2. Narration (Rhetoric)
I. Title
840.9′008   PQ295.N/

Library of Congress cataloguing in publication data
Wing, Nathaniel, 1938–
The limits of narrative.
(Cambridge studies in French)
Bibliography.
Includes index.
1. French literature – 19th century – History and criticism.
2. Narration (Rhetoric)   I. Title.   II. Series.
PQ295.N18W56   1986   840′.9′008   86-6114

ISBN 0 521 30710 4

For Betsy

CONTENTS

ACKNOWLEDGEMENTS

I wish to acknowledge the encouragement and helpful criticism of colleagues and friends who discussed this project with me in the various stages of its writing. Thanks go to my associates at Miami University who read and commented on several chapters of the book, Jim Creech, Jane Gallop, Peggy Kamuf and especially to Marie-Claire Vallois and Mitchell Greenberg for their attentive readings of the entire manuscript and for their warm support. I also wish to express my gratitude to Ross Chambers for his interest in this book and for his generous endorsement of my work in past years. Janet Mercer's unfailing cooperation in typing various versions of these chapters is also acknowledged gratefully. Finally, my wife Betsy assisted me in so many ways, from helpful discussions of my arguments to insightful readings of each chapter; she has been a constant advisor and critic.

GENERAL EDITOR'S PREFACE

This series aims at providing a new forum for the discussion of major critical or scholarly topics within the field of French studies. It differs from most similar-seeming ventures in the degree of freedom which contributing authors are allowed and in the range of subjects covered. For the series is not concerned to promote any single area of academic specialisation or any single theoretical approach. Authors are invited to address themselves to *problems*, and to argue their solutions in whatever terms seem best able to produce an incisive and cogent account of the matter in hand. The search for such terms will sometimes involve the crossing of boundaries between familiar academic disciplines, or the calling of those boundaries into dispute. Most of the studies will be written especially for the series, although from time to time it will also provide new editions of outstanding works which were previously out of print, or originally published in languages other than English or French.

INTRODUCTION

... l'homme a composé sa propre figure dans les interstices d'un langage en fragments.   M. Foucault, *Les Mots et les Choses*[1]

L'Oeuvre pure implique la disparition élocutoire du poète, qui cède l'initiative aux mots, par la heurt de leur inégalité mobilisés; ils s'allument de reflets réciproques comme une virtuelle traînée de feux sur des pierreries, remplaçant la respiration perceptible en l'ancien souffle lyrique ou la direction personnel enthousiaste de la phrase.

                           S. Mallarmé, "Crise de vers"[2]

In 1886 Mallarmé announced a profound shift in the ways that writing can consider literature. The elusive formulations of "Crise de vers" are often taken as a series of propositions which constitute our modernity; the text is situated as the threshold of the contemporary moment. If not precisely false, this interpretation is in many ways untrue, even mystified. In pronouncing the death of a poet, the irreconcilable retreat of the subject and its re-emergence in the transpositions of language, Mallarmé's text is engaged in a general reflection about the incompatibility between man's being, the nature of things and language which has many analogs in other post-Romantic writers. The break, then, which Mallarmé announced and which the text itself performs in the configurations of its language is only possible as a repetition of an intense questioning in the nineteenth century about how the known and the unknown can be thought, about the desiring and speculating subject, about the retreat of origins, the discontinuities and fragmentation of language. In short, Mallarmé's text has a history; to situate "Crise de vers" as a beginning and to accord to its speculations the status of reflections of modernity is to forget this history. One can re-read Mallarmé's prose, however, as a figure of modernity if it is acknowledged that this is possible only against a background of the already begun.

While the problems raised in 1886 in Mallarmé's speculations

1

Introduction

about writing are unfolded in configurations specific to that text, they are also the questions which emerge consistently from the readings of Baudelaire, Flaubert, Rimbaud and an earlier Mallarmé in the chapters which follow. Put most generally, the question is how thought, desire and the fictions of experiences are articulated in the unbridgeable gap which separates the figure of a subject present to itself and what is irreducibly other, the unthought, the unthinkable. The exploration of these problems in fiction does not proceed from the stable ground of an integral subject nor lead to a confirmation of being, but rather opens up a series of questions about the question of being.[3] Writing is no longer lodged within the limits of representation and emerges from the order of representation at the expense of the fiction of an integral self. The depersonalization of the writers is concurrent with a disintegration of the links between language, thought and things:

Abolie, la prétention, esthétiquement une erreur, quoique'elle régît les chefs-d'oeuvre, d'inclure au papier subtil du volume autre chose que par exemple l'horreur de la forêt, ou la tonnerre muet épars au feuillage; non le bois intrinsèque et dense des arbres.

. . .

Parler n'a trait à la réalité des choses que commercialement: en littérature, cela se contente d'y faire allusion ou de distraire leur qualité qu'incorpera quelque idée . . .

Cette visée, je la dis Transposition – Structure, une autre.   (365–6)

The urgency with which literature scrutinizes itself in Mallarmé's later writings ("l'acte d'écrire se scruta jusqu'en l'origine")[4] is already inscribed in each of the earlier texts that will concern us here: Baudelaire's *Les Fleurs du mal* and *Le Spleen de Paris*, Flaubert's *Madame Bovary*, Rimbaud's *Une Saison en enfer* and Mallarmé's "L'Après-midi d'un faune". Though with varying degrees of indirection, these texts explore certain rhetorical and ontological impasses; these are reiterated as unresolvable, yet deflected as the texts drift away from identity and open up radically new modes of writing and understanding. By demystifying the figure of romantic subjectivity these fictions disengage veiled differences and repressed hierarchies in oppositions between subject/object, self/other, masculine/feminine, teller/told, and others which circulate within the myth of the "proper" or "self-same." To the extent that these texts ironically or nostalgically repeat aspects of the myth they deconstruct, they produce violence within that containment; there is a heavy residue of desire for unity of consciousness present to itself as subjectivity, for an ultimate congruity between sign and meaning, for a fusion between desire and its objects. Yet, in the dismembered lyric "self" of Baudelaire's verse allegories, in the ex-centric narrators of his prose poetry, in Flaubert's demystification of Emma's narratives of Romantic desire, in the dispersal of the "absolutely modern" narrating subject severed from history in Rimbaud's *Une Saison en enfer* and in the "false confusions" between narrative, dream and the fictions of desire in "L'Après-midi d'un faune," the desires for limits, for unity and for a language capable of securing the self-same are shown to be lures. In various ways, the most evident of which takes the narrator as its central figure and the forms of narrative as its rhetorical support, these texts explore the impulses for containment of meaning, for the authority over expression: as they draw out the impasses produced, they open up on new configurations of subjectivity and meaning, less destructively violent, charged by a different excess.

Each chapter of this book focuses on particular rhetorical figures and narrative patterns and proposes a reading of a specific literary corpus.

The opposition in Baudelaire's esthetics between allegory and symbol is examined in Chapter 1, in several poems of *Les Fleurs du mal* in which allegory functions in ways radically different from those outlined by the theoretical texts. Baudelaire's theoretical writings privilege the symbolic mode over allegory as a poetic language of concrete intuition, named variously as symbol, correspondence, universal analogy or *surnaturalisme*. Consistent with Romantic esthetics, allegory is discredited as a rational, even prosaic mode of expression which differs from the processes of universal analogy in its function and its finality. In spite of Baudelaire's devaluation of allegory, however, it is one of the most prevalent figures of *Les Fleurs du mal*. In "Le Masque," the transparency of an allegorical enigma is revealed with ironic astonishment as the allegorical signified is unveiled, yet the control of meaning is itself subjected to irony. In "Le Cygne," "Les Sept Vieillards" and "Le Tonneau de la haine," allegory momentarily effects a recuperation of sense, hidden and controlled by the figural system, only to be caught in a vertiginous and virtually limitless multiplication of meaning in an open displacement. The allegory of the Danaides' Vessel serves as a figure of the figure; there is an irresistible imperative to contain meaning, to fill the figure with its own sense, yet meaning always exceeds the limits of containment.

"On certain relations: figures of sexuality in Baudelaire" considers a number of problems opened up with particular force by Baudelaire's texts as the notion of *genre* (in its rhetorical and sexual senses) becomes unstable: these problems are the figuration of objects of desire or aversion, specifically the figuration of sexuality. I examine several passages on love and art in Baudelaire's journals, "Fusées" and "Mon Coeur mis à nu," a text on woman in the essay *Le Peintre de la vie moderne*, and the preface to the prose poems, *Le Spleen de Paris*. These readings provide an interpretive network for consideration of several of the prose poems.

On the one hand Baudelaire's figuration of sexuality is consistent with that of a nineteenth-century male imaginary in advancing hierarchical oppositions in certain texts, while on the other hand other texts dismantle those oppositions. Sexuality is often defined through oppositions in which the "mystery of woman," paradigm of enigmatic difference, is accessible to an interpreting male subject in terms which attempt to appropriate feminine otherness. Many of Baudelaire's texts, however, exceed a dialectics between subject and object, disrupt polarities and produce an intensely pleasurable circulation of meanings and erotic energy. A metaphoric mode of figuring objects of desire, as a double of the poet or a feminine analog, stills desire or erupts in violence; metonymic figures of partial objects, however, proliferate desire and intimately associate erotic pleasure with the production of poetry.

"Emma's stories: narrative, repetition and desire in *Madame Bovary*," re-examines the familiar problem of irony in the novel in a discussion of Emma's stories of Romantic desire. Flaubert's use of narrative in the novel demystifies in many ways the desires which motivate Emma's stories, her fantasies, dreams and her extended fictions of escape and romantic love. Her narratives, protonarratives (fantasies and dreams) and her letters to her lovers can be read as repeated and unsuccessful attempts to give order to desires which are destabilizing in their effects and ultimately unattainable.

The division between language and experience is a major concern of the novel. Emma's stories oppose the events which constitute her world, yet lack the force to transform that world. One can attribute Emma's difficulties throughout the novel, then, not just to her foolishness and to the mediocrity of her milieu, but to the more general problems of desire and its realization, of language and illusion.

This chapter focuses on the content of the order of Emma's narratives; it also re-examines the general problematic of writing in the novel. If Emma is a figure for the writer at a certain point in the history of the novel, this figure does not function exclusively as an uncomplex emblem of the deluded Romantic in an already post-Romantic moment. In fact, the novel does not validate without reserve the control of an enlightened narrator whose understanding transcends the dilemmas of Romantic subjectivity and Romantic literary stereotypes. An omniscient narrator is also caught up in an intricate web of repetition and difference which both includes and radically exceeds identification between narrator and protagonist, includes and exceeds a simple demystification which would deny altogether the links between protagonist and narrator.

"The autobiography of rhetoric: on reading Rimbaud's *Une Saison en enfer*" analyzes confession as an interpretive process in which examination of the narrator's past and present, of history, metaphysics, love and writing leads with increasing explicitness to an examination of the speaking subject as a configuration of language. The narrator is also a reader whose interest in the course of the poem shifts from an interpretation of a narrative signified (*histoire*) to an evaluation of narration (*discours*). In many respects, the poem conforms to traditional patterns of auto-biography; it tells a story of a passage through a world of past sufferings, delusions and failed strategies to reinvent love and art, from which the poet emerges into the clear light of truth ("Matin") as the narrated self and narrating *I* merge in the present of narration. The poet overcomes a deficient ("pagan") language, rejects a personal and cultural history in which he has no place and seeks absolute newness ("Il faut être absolument moderne"). The narrating subject is engaged less in a process of self-realization, however, than in writing the self in and as language, deprived of any reassuring epistemological or ontological ground. This chapter studies the narrative patterns of the poem, specifically the uses of verb tenses and the interaction between narration and the narrated past; it considers the implications of the imperative to be "absolutely modern" in terms of relations between history, language and a fragmented "subject."

The narrator of Mallarmé's "L'Après-midi d'un faune" purports to wish to "perpetuate" two nymphs, to possess them sexually and to reproduce the story of his own desire. "False confusions: fictions of masculine desire in Mallarmé's 'L'Après-midi d'un faune'" studies the distinctions between subject and object and the possibility of appropriating an erotic object; the poem suggests that there are radical and irreconcilable differences between feminine pleasure and masculine desire which unravel the faun's complex narrative.

The narrator's own story fails to establish limits between memory, present interpretation and invention. As the faun's monologue unfolds, it becomes apparent that an "authentic" narrative of desire is impossible, that whatever fragments of "real," past events may endure are available only through a figural language which blurs the demarcation between the "real" and fantasy, and collapses essential temporal separations between past, present and future. This chapter studies the disruptions of the distinctions between literal and figurative language, the use of personal pronouns, particularly the doubling of the narrating voice as both *I* and *you*, self and other, and the abolition of the distinction between the first and third person (the so-called non-person) as the faun's thoughts and song are metaphorized and inscribed as decor at once external to and formative of the "subject." The study also considers how this text from Mallarmé's early writing (roughly, 1865–76) prefigures practices which will be systematically developed in the later poems and in the later critical texts.

In the place of a conclusion, a final chapter "The trials of authority under Louis Bonaparte" speculates on the wider, historical context of the textual practices discussed in the book. I explore the configurations of certain fissures in the symbolic system of political representation, in a reading of Marx's writings on the consolidation of power by Louis Bonaparte, *Class Struggles in France: 1848–1850* and *The 18th Brumaire of Louis Bonaparte* and in a discussion of the documents of Flaubert's and Baudelaire's trials for "outrages to public morality," in 1857. The decentering and fragmentation of the subject, the disruption of hierarchical relations between prose and poetry, narrator and protagonist, masculine and feminine, and so on, and the disordering of narrative *telos* in fiction are associated here with a wider crisis in cultural systems of representation. This chapter attempts to set the context for a more extensive inquiry into the conjunction between discursive registers, the literary and the historical, and into the ideological status of literary texts, which both reproduce dominant culture and subvert the dominant which inhabits them. While this inquiry into complex and interrelated levels of discourse is necessarily hypothetical and without any claim to having established relations of determination, it is hoped that it will open up questions about the interaction between politics, ideology and fiction.

At issue throughout this book are the ways in which literary texts question their own relations to mastery and to a desire for totalization, which is never fully renounced, yet always deflected and displaced as it is reiterated. A brief quotation from an early essay by Roland Barthes, "Littérature et signification," will serve as a guide to what follows, to be recalled at the end of this text, when I explore the wider issues concerning writing and history:

en littérature ... il n'y a pas de question *pure*: une question n'est jamais que sa propre réponse éparse, dispersée en fragments entre lesquels le sens fuse et fuit tout à la fois.[5]

1

THE DANAIDES VESSEL: ON READING BAUDELAIRE'S ALLEGORIES

An inquiry which proposes to re-examine the functions of allegory in *Les Fleurs du mal* risks, at the outset, recalling with particular insistence that most famous of Baudelaire's allegorical personifications, the delicate monster in "Au lecteur," *L'Ennui*, who threatens to engulf the world in a vast yawn. Conventional poetic devices, at least since the mid-nineteenth century, are not held in good repute, in so far as they have been associated with normative rhetoric and with the use of figurative language as an "ornament of discourse." In reconsidering Baudelaire's allegories we risk participating in that condescension with which recent history has treated the figure. There is a profusion of allegory, however, in *Les Fleurs du mal* which cannot be written off simply, as Valéry and others would have it, as a repeated lapse into an outmoded eloquence, or as sententious and moralistic posturing.[1] Furthermore, Baudelaire often praises the figure unequivocally as:

ce genre si *spirituel*, que les peintres maladroits nous ont accoutumés à mépriser, est vraiment l'une des formes primitives et les plus naturelles de la poésie[2]

In the familiar late eighteenth-century and Romantic schema, allegory as a figural transfer of meaning is eclipsed in importance by symbol, which comes to stand for processes of analogy functioning within a radical monism. The problem of allegorical constructs in *Les Fleurs du mal* is considerably more complex than this opposition between symbol and allegory would lead us to believe. Our reading cannot place itself *outside* of the debate, however. That controversy, which inextricably mixes considerations about language with metaphysics and esthetics, necessarily informs a reading of the poems. Because its delimiting concepts are also to be found in those texts, in the art and literary criticism and the *Journaux intimes*, it is appropriate to review it briefly here.[3] The esthetic devaluation of allegory, furthermore, is the source of irony in many

8

of *Les Fleurs du mal*, in which the texts play with and against a shop-worn rhetorical figure. Within a certain esthetic and metaphysical enclosure, however, concepts are frequently turned against themselves and their presuppositions undermined by processes of meaning which cannot be accounted for by the traditional rhetorical/esthetic definitions. My inquiry will consider the interplay between these configurations of meaning.

For Baudelaire, the term *symbol* frequently stands for figurative language in general; it is assumed to be capable of transforming all individual experience into general truth, since, as de Man summarizes:

The subjectivity of experience is preserved when it is translated into language; the world is then no longer seen as a configuration of entities that designate a plurality of distinct and isolated meanings, but as a configuration of symbols ultimately leading to a total, single, and universal meaning.[4]

The numerous passages which Baudelaire devotes to symbol give a privileged status to the symbolic mode as the poetic language of concrete intuition, designated by various interchangeable expressions, such as *symbole, correspondance, analogie universelle* and *surnaturalisme*. Allegory, on the other hand, as the morpheme *allos* (other) indicates, differs from the process of universal analogy in both its function and its finality. It relays meaning from one semantic level to another, within a limited polyvalence. The suggestiveness of allegory in art is criticized as too rationally mechanical, exhausted as soon as the meaning (signified) is attained.

The short essay on "L'Art philosophique" (1859) formulates this contrast succinctly and in terms sufficiently general to apply equally well to painting or literary language. Baudelaire reproaches philosophical, pictorial art for meddling in concerns which are properly those of didactic prose, by seeking to replace the book and to teach history, morality and philosophy.

Toute bonne sculpture, toute bonne peinture, toute bonne musique, suggère les sentiments, et les rêveries qu'elle veut suggérer.

Mais le raisonnement, la déduction, appartiennent au livre.

Ainsi l'art philosophique est un retour vers l'imagerie nécessaire à l'enfance des peuples, et s'il était rigoureusement fidèle à lui-même, il s'astreindrait à juxtaposer autant d'images successives qu'il en est contenu dans une phrase quelconque qu'il voudrait exprimer.

. . .

Plus l'art voudra être philosophiquement clair, plus il se dégradera et remontera vers l'hiéroglyphe enfantin; ... (1099–100)

As an example of the aberration, Baudelaire describes in detail a representation of *une bonne mort*, a virtuous man surprised in his sleep by death; each figural element in the painting is correlated with an extrinsic meaning:

Il faut, dans la traduction des oeuvres d'art philosophiques, apporter une grande minutie et une grande attention; là les lieux, le décor, les meubles, les ustensiles (voir Hogarth), tout est allégorie, allusion, hiéroglyphes, rébus. (1101)[5]

Both the separation of levels of meaning and the rational link between them provoke Baudelaire's criticism, for in this mode the signifier is cut off from a (mythical) consubstantial relationship between the sensible and the non-sensible, which would obtain in the symbolic mode of "pure," "modern" art. The conventionalized relay between levels of meaning in allegory both maintains a separation of the levels and claims to link them conceptually through a translation. In terms of contemporary semiotics, the first level of meaning is constituted by the link between a signifier and a signified and subsequently becomes a signifier for a secondary signified.

Allegory thus functions through its parallel systems as both a referral and deferral of meaning; in positing and incorporating a second semantic level, it can be recognized as a figure of containment. As such, it is inimical to that expansion of meaning in the symbolic mode through universal analogy, which, for Baudelaire, is virtually limitless multiplicity and concentration of being produced by the associative potential of language. The opening paragraph of "L'Art philosophique" briefly states that ideal:

Qu'est-ce que l'art pur suivant la conception moderne? C'est créer une magie suggestive contenant à la fois l'objet et le sujet, le monde extérieur à l'artiste et l'artiste lui-même. (1099)

In this passage, characteristic elements of the symbolic mode are a fusion between the semantic and representative functions of language, in analogy, an abolition of the distinctions between the particular and the general, and a synthesis between subject and object in a relation of simultaneity.[6]

I return to these distinctions because, as I have noted, they function according to the schema outlined in many of Baudelaire's poems and because they are undercut in others by certain textual processes. Furthermore, the terms in which a discussion of the figures is necessarily formulated, binary relationships (semantic or intersubjective), separation between levels of meaning, and a temporal dialectic between interconnected sign systems lead to a reconsideration of the problems of duality in Baudelaire, to a re-examination of meaning, not as a system of containment, but as an irreducible and genetic multiplicity.[7] Finally, these questions invite us to look again at the still tantalizing problem of ironies in Baudelaire.

This reading will not propose an all-inclusive typology of allegory in Baudelaire's verse. A comprehensive system as a totalizing discourse, whether that of the poetic or critical text, is subject to suspicion as Baudelaire notes in a passage written in 1855:

un système est une espèce de damnation qui nous pousse à une abjuration perpétuelle; il en faut toujours inventer un autre, et cette fatigue est un cruel châtiment. Et toujours mon système était beau, vaste, spacieux, commode, propre et lisse surtout . . .

("L'Exposition universelle de 1855," 955)

In various ways, however, the question of control is central to the inquiry, as each text manipulates and undermines allegory as a figure that delimits and masters meaning. In "Le Masque," the opacity or transparency of an allegorical enigma is unveiled with ironic astonishment as the allegorical signified is revealed, yet that ironic control of meaning is itself subjected to irony by the text. In a second group of poems, "Le Cygne," "Les Sept Vieillards" and "Le Tonneau de la haine," allegory momentarily recuperates meaning, hidden and controlled by the figural system, only to be caught in a vertiginous and virtually limitless multiplication of signification in a process of production and open displacement. Irony in this second group of texts is far more unsettling than in the first; it is a delirium verging on madness.

"Le Masque," in "Spleen et Idéal," is dedicated to the sculptor Ernest Christophe, and subtitled "Statue allégorique dans le Goût de la Renaissance." The poem describes a statue of a woman in a profusion of visual detail commensurate with the physical abundance of the model:

> Contemplons ce trésor de grâces florentines;
> Dans l'ondulation de ce corps musculeux
> L'Elégance et la Force abondent, soeurs divines.
> Cette femme, morceau vraiment miraculeux,

11

Divinement robuste, adorablement mince,
Est faite pour trôner sur des lits somptueux,
Et charmer les loisirs d'un pontife ou d'un prince.

Her gaze is a combination of fatuousness, languor and mockery:

– Aussi, vois ce souris fin et voluptueux
Où la Fatuité promène son extase;
Ce long regard sournois, langoureux et moqueur;
Ce visage mignard, tout encadré de gaze,
Dont chaque trait nous dit avec un air vainqueur:
"La Volupté m'appelle et l'Amour me couronne!"

   Both narrator and reader are set in the text as spectators and, as the Poet invites the reader to approach the statue, the narrator, in a series of hyperboles, proclaims astonishment at the deception of Art ("O blasphème de l'art! ô surprise fatale!"). The voluptuous face is only a mask, the statue of a two-headed monster:

La femme au corps divin, promettant le bonheur,
Par le haut se termine en monstre bicéphale!

A parallel series of terms unequivocally designating the artistic travesty of truth (*masque, décor suborneur, le visage qui ment*) and those which identify the "true representation" ("La véritable tête, et la sincère face") point unmistakably to the dual structure of meaning in allegory:

– Mais non! ce n'est qu'un masque, un décor suborneur,
Ce visage éclairé d'une exquise grimace,
Et, regarde, voici, crispée atrocement,
La véritable tête, et la sincère face
Renversée à l'abri de la face qui ment.

The enigma is posed explicitly: "Mais pourquoi pleure-t-elle? Elle, beauté parfaite . . ." and answered three lines below, as the key to the allegory is provided:

– Elle pleure, insensé, parce qu'elle a vécu!
Et parce qu'elle vit! Mais ce qu'elle déplore
Surtout, ce qui la fait frémir jusqu'aux genoux,
C'est que demain, hélas! il faudra vivre encore!
Demain, après-demain et toujours! – comme nous!

The poem contains elements of surprise and mystery, which in Baudelaire's esthetic are necessary to artistic effect, and which are inscribed throughout *Les Fleurs du mal*. These effects are ironized here, however, by their very explicitness, by the mock exaggeration of surprise and by the singularly direct question and answer format in which the moral of the fable is presented. In this way the text plays ironically with the dual, even two-faced structure of allegory, with both the initially enigmatic distance between levels of meaning and the necessarily rational correlation between those levels. A reading of the poem which would delimit the ironic effects to this implicit devaluation of a didactic rhetorical figure could be substantiated by reference to Baudelaire's comments on sculpture in the "Salons" of 1846 and 1859. In the section "Pourquoi la sculpture est ennuyeuse" of the "Salon of 1846," sculpture is criticized as either too primitive ("un art de Caraïbes") or too naively mimetic. In the "Salon of 1859," Baudelaire discusses the statue by Christophe which was the model for this text noting that:

Le caractère vigoureux du corps fait un constraste pittoresque avec l'expression mystique d'une idée toute mondaine, et la surprise n'y joue pas un rôle plus important qu'il n'est permis. (1095)

In both the poem and the prose analysis, effects of surprise, allegory of irony, are strictly controlled. To delimit allegory and irony in "Le Masque" in this manner is to read them as vehicles of containment. This is true in part, of course, but one may question whether the moral is that simple and explore the possibility that a critique of the irony of containment is already at work in the text. A re-examination of the final stanza suggests that the ironic distance between the poet/reader/spectator of the allegory and the allegorical signified is itself the subject of irony. The accumulation of logical connectors, the periodic syntax of the conclusion ("Mais ce qu'elle déplore / Surtout, ce qui la fait frémir ... C'est que ...") seem to posit the truth of the text very much in the manner of those literal translations of philosophical art that Baudelaire criticized elsewhere. The final words of the poem, however, ("comme nous!"), unexpectedly narrow the distance between the message figured by the allegorical statue and the reader/spectator as judge, by including both the reader and the poet as protagonists in the same metaphysical conflict as that conveyed by the allegory. The clear conscience of ironic containment is itself the subject of irony through the revelation that it is a mystified consciousness. There is thus a far more complex and indeterminate interplay of irony here than our initial reading anticipated, and one which links the metaphysical dilemma allegorized by the text to the *structure* of allegory. The meaning constituted by the allegorical system can consist, as de Man has shown, only "in a repetition of a previous sign with which it can never coincide, since it is of the essence of this previous sign to be pure anteriority."[8] Meaning is structured here as a process of deferral. An indefinite temporal displacement of sense is oriented simultaneously in two directions: the meaning of the allegory depends upon a previous sign, the first face of the statue derives its meaning from the second, the face of suffering. Yet the discovery of that second face does not delimit meaning in a stable manner, but projects it as irony in a displacement toward an indefinite future (*encore*).

The initial interplay between allegory and esthetic conventions is less marked in several other texts of *Les Fleurs du mal*, in which meaning subverts the traditional mode of allegory as a figure of containment and concurrently undermines the status of the textual first person as a stable subject. I will outline this problematic in readings of "Le Cygne," "Les Sept Vieillards" and "Le Tonneau de la haine."

The allegorical signified in "Le Cygne" is introduced in the opening line of the poem, and thereby reinforces the traditionally rational connection between the two levels of meaning:

> Andromaque, je pense à vous! Ce petit fleuve,
> Pauvre et triste miroir où jadis resplendit
> L'immense majesté de vos douleurs de veuve,
> Ce Simoïs menteur qui par vos pleurs grandit,
>
> A fécondé soudain ma mémoire fertile,
> Comme je traversais le nouveau Carrousel.

A link between the decor, and by extension, the forthcoming narrative anecdote, is established as a correlation between signifieds, in which an immediate experience is *read* by the Poet as the relay of an anterior meaning. The first section of the poem describes a construction site at the Nouveau Carrousel, which figures in its rapid change and disorder the instability of the heart. An analeptic narrative then recalls an earlier scene in which a swan had escaped from its cage in a menagerie since destroyed. This allegory of exile is too well known to require elucidation here; my main interest is in the interrelation between allegories in the two sections of the poem. In the first, the figure clearly functions within a circumscribed polyvalence, in the traditional manner, while the second part of the text puts in question the possibility of that very containment of meaning. The opening stanza of the second section repeats the descriptive framework and returns explicitly to the

Poet/observer as interpreter of the allegorical landscape, in an apparent reassertion of his mastery over meanings:

> Paris change! mais rien dans ma mélancholie
> N'a bougé! palais neufs, échafaudages, blocs,
> Vieux faubourgs, tout pour moi devient allégorie,
> Et mes chers souvenirs sont plus lourds que des rocs.

The exclamation "tout pour moi devient allégorie" may be read initially as a rather conventional hyperbole exalting the Poet's capacity to decipher the world; read "dans tous les sens," however, as Baudelaire counsels elsewhere, and read in its context, it is hardly a reassuring statement, as it precedes an enumeration of no fewer than *nine* allegorical figures in a series which remains *open*.[9] This serial acceleration of meaning produces a radical loosening of the relationship between the signifier and signified, suggesting the terrifying possibility that any person, object or relationship can mean absolutely anything.

An anaphoric sequence, structured as a repetition of the verbal unit *je pense à* ... presents the series of synonymous figures: a negress, nostalgic for "la superbe Afrique"; an indefinite "quiconque a perdu ce qui ne se retrouve / Jamais, jamais!"; those who nurse suffering like a she wolf; orphans; the Poet's own memory, which sounds like a horn in the forest; sailors forgotten on an island; captives; the vanquished; and, finally, an indefinite "à bien d'autres encore," which leaves the series perpetually open resonating in an infinite echo (*cor, encor*). The supposedly rational, monosemic or polysemic figure functions, then, in a curious and unsettling manner, to inscribe the predicament of a thought caught in an open and endless displacement. Poetic thought is no longer delimited by the semantic horizon of the allegorical signified; it breaks that horizon by the repetition of an endless discontinuity. Each allegorical figure reiterates the impossibility of retrieving a lost origin; the loss which is allegorized here is that which is always already absent. The "object" ("ce qui ne se retrouve jamais ..."), moreover, is not easily compensated for by the language which figures its displacement, for language is here powerless to restore the plenitude of an original presence.

The following poem in "Les Tableaux parisiens," "Les Sept Vieillards," to which I will allude only briefly, carries one step further the process of displacing meaning in an allegorical system, and that is the step into madness. To think the reiteration of an allegorical figure as a repetition cut from any link to a signified, as

15

origin of its own replication "Sosie inexorable ... Dégoûtant Phénix, fils et père de lui-même ..." is to think the production of sense as non-sense. There is no nostalgia here for a lost plenitude, an absence which is the deluded form of presence, but its ultimate guarantor. In the pure interplay of allegorical signifiers, the poem provokes the terror of non-sense, as an attack on the formation of meaning. As the Poet encounters:

> ... un vieillard dont les guenilles jaunes
> Imitaient la couleur de ce ciel pluvieux,
> Et dont l'aspect aurait fait pleuvoir les aumônes,
> Sans la méchanceté qui luisait dans ses yeux, ...

he is assaulted by a series of baroque spectres; the old man appears seven times:

> Car je comptai sept fois, de minute en minute,
> Ce sinistre vieillard qui se multipliait!

Here the enigma is not formulated as a sense veiled by the allegory; the mystery is the meaning of repetition. Again the Poet is the *reader* of the allegory, but what he seeks to interpret is the process of its proliferation.

An extension of the completed cycle of seven would leap into infinity:

> Aurais-je, sans mourir, contemplé le huitième,
> Sosie inexorable, ironique et fatal,
> Dégoûtant Phénix, fils et père de lui-même?
> – Mais je tournai le dos au cortège infernal.

Death menaces the Poet at the moment that the proliferation threatens to become engaged in an infinite spiral. Exasperated, he turns away from the allegorical scene to take refuge in his room, hoping to recover his reason; the solace that he finds there, however, is the delirium of madness:

> Vainement ma raison voulait prendre la barre;
> La tempête en jouant déroutait ses efforts,
> Et mon âme dansait, dansait vieille gabarre
> Sans mâts, sur une mer monstrueuse et sans bords!

Repetition is both the insistence of meaning and its impossibility within the enclosure of a system that requires meaning to circulate as the sense *of* something. That need is figured here by the allegorical decor, by the poet as reader, by the intimate space of the room, even by the anticipated, but absent, limits of the sea. Madness begins where reason contemplates pure gratuitousness, and in this text that is the undoing of the first person as a subject. That gratuitousness, however, is an uncanny repetition; as the allegory escapes the control of the subject/reader there is a terrifying shift in the functional value of the allegory from a figure of containment to a figure of the uncontrollable return of the fearful. The rhetoric of mastery is violently displaced by the unfathomable rhetoric of madness.[10]

"Le Tonneau de la haine," the last text I shall consider, takes the myth of the Danaides' vessel as its "literal" level. The vat which the daughters of Danaus were condemned to fill as punishment for having slaughtered their bridgerooms on their wedding night is allegorized here as Hate. The role of the Danaides is taken by Vengeance, who:

> A beau précipiter dans ses ténèbres vides
> De grands seaux pleins du sang et des larmes des morts, . . .

and it is the Devil who pokes holes in the vat through which flow the blood and tears:

> Le Démon fait des trous secrets à ces abîmes,
> Par où fuiraient mille ans de sueurs et d'efforts,
> Quand même elle saurait ranimer ses victimes,
> Et pour les pressurer resusciter leurs corps.

This overfilling, which is both an excess (there is too much to be contained), and a deficiency (the container cannot fully enclose), repeats a process figured in "Le Cygne" and in "Les Sept Vieillards." Once again, this endless proliferation is a very threatening indeterminacy, for what is figured here is the loss of the illusion of meaning. Containment, fullness, completion are necessary, since the buckets are themselves being filled and continually being emptied into the vat, but the process is inadequate to the task. Allegory thus inscribes the impossibility of figurative language to contain what it would hold.

This allegory of indeterminacy is doubled in the tercets by a second allegory, this time presenting Hate as a drunkard whose thirst multiplies with its satisfaction. An unhappy boozer, Hate can never know oblivion by passing out under the table:

> La Haine est un ivrogne au fond d'une taverne,
> Qui sent toujours la soif naître de la liqueur
> Et se multiplier comme l'hydre de Lerne.

> – Mais les buveurs heureux connaissent leur vainqueur,
> Et la Haine est vouée à ce sort lamentable
> De ne pouvoir jamais s'endormir sous la table.

The tragically grotesque image of Hate in the final tercet not only reiterates the characterization of desire (Hate) as seeking an object endlessly displaced, but it ironizes in a most deprecatory manner the ironic consciousness. The self-multiplication which forms the ironic interruption of being is written elsewhere as a process of demystification asserted, as in "L'Héautontimorouménos" as a lucid sado-masochistic doubling of the self, both victim and torturer, wound and knife:

> Je suis la plaie et le couteau!
> Je suis le soufflet et la joue!
> Je suis les membres et la roue,
> Et la victime et le bourreau!

In "L'Irrémédiable," irony is figured as consciousness contemplating its own fragmentation:

> Tête-à-tête sombre et limpide
> Qu'un coeur devenu son miroir!

In "Le Tonneau de la haine," however, desire's victim cannot turn awareness of the predicament into an investigation of inauthenticity. In an interplay between irony and allegory, meaning as a process of positing and circumscribing effects of sense is interrupted and indefinitely deferred. In the quatrains of the poem a figure of allegory both calls for and denies the possibility of sense. The text also inscribes *irony* as a turning away of meaning by figuring a poetic language discontinuous with its own telos. Where he anticipates rhetorical constructs which deflect, yet ultimately reappropriate meanings, the reader is engaged by and in the writing of a limitless deferral, which demystifies some of Baudelaire's most persistent myths.

2

ON CERTAIN RELATIONS:
FIGURES OF SEXUALITY IN
BAUDELAIRE

The problem of difference among genres and within literary language, as critics have noted, is raised explicitly by the formula: prose poem, even though, for contemporary readers it has lost much of its force as an oxymoron. In his preface to *Le Spleen de Paris*, Baudelaire alludes to these differences within the framework of a presumed understanding of the generic specificity of poetry:

Quel est celui de nous qui n'a pas, dans ses jours d'ambition, rêvé le miracle d'une prose poétique, musicale sans rythme et sans rime, assez souple et assez heurtée pour s'adapter aux mouvements lyriques de l'âme, aux ondulations de la rêverie, aux soubresauts de la conscience?[1]   (229)

We needn't linger over the passage to note that it does not advance what it would seem to promise, a poetics of prose poetry, but poses a question which remains suspended, unresolved. That famous formula doesn't define much of anything. In its characterization of prose, the passage quickly shifts from rhetorical terms ("musicale sans rythme et sans rime") to rhetorical figures ("ondulations de la rêverie ... soubresauts de la conscience") more appropriate, conventionally, to the language of literature, especially to poetry, than to the metalanguage of an analytic discourse. It is more helpful, perhaps, to consider the paragraph in terms of the relations between differences which it sets in play. Barbara Johnson, in her *Défigurations du langage poétique*, has shown that this passage, and the prose poems themselves, invite us to reconsider the question of difference beyond a simple dyadic opposition between poetry and prose.[2] The element of this pair which is assumed to be marked metalinguistically, poetry, is no longer set simply over and against an unmarked term: prose. By stating that it is non-poetry, and by asserting itself as prose, the prose poem produces the meta-linguistic mark which traditionally belongs to poetry and thus shifts consideration to the interaction between two literary codes. A well-established polarity is short-circuited and dysfunctions. I don't

19

wish to retrace here what Barbara Johnson has articulated so well, but to begin an inquiry into other differences, distinct in many ways from those she has written about. In this chapter I will consider a number of problems opened up with particular force in Baudelaire's texts as the notion of genre becomes unstable, that is, the problems of the figuration of objects of desire, or aversion, and more specifically, the figuration of sexuality. I will examine several passages from the *Journaux intimes*, a text on woman in the essay on Constantin Guys, "Le Peintre de la vie moderne," and the preface to *Le Spleen de Paris*. My reading of these texts will provide an interpretive network for a consideration of several of the prose poems. In brief, just as considerations on the literarity of the prose poem shift away from terms set in opposition, Baudelaire's figuration of sexuality both advances hierarchical oppositions in certain texts and, in others, problematizes and even deconstructs those oppositions. We turn from differences between terms to differences among terms whose meaning is produced by their plurality and instability. First I will attempt to articulate some of the problems produced by certain definitions of sexuality and art; how these impasses are deflected in an extension of erotic activity will be traced later in discussion of some of the prose poems, such as "Le Thyrse," "Les Projets," "Les Fenêtres" and "Les Foules."

With characteristic inconsistency, Baudelaire formulates the terms of sexual difference in remarkably contrasting and incompatible ways. On the one hand, sexuality is defined in a manner congruent with a nineteenth-century male imaginary through oppositions in which the "mystery of women," the paradigm of enigmatic difference, becomes accessible to an interpreting male subject in terms which ultimately attempt to appropriate feminine otherness. A construction of male "identity" is projected within a dyadic structure in which an explicit or veiled hierarchy obliterates difference.[3] On the other hand, many texts exceed a dialectics of desire between subject and object, deconstruct polarities and produce a circulation of meanings and an explosion ("Le Vieux Saltimbanque") of intense pleasure. Here we can trace the play of sexuality as a circulation of difference, multiple, unstable and beyond the reach of appropriation. Enjoyment is produced by difference which exceeds subject or object, named variously as "des jouissances fiévreuses" ("Les Foules") or "l'explosion frénétique de la vitalité" ("Le Vieux Saltimbanque").

Figures of sexual difference always engage Baudelaire's narrator in seeking and interpreting that intense pleasure or intoxication which, we are repeatedly told, is produced by the text act. Nowhere in Baudelaire's writings are the complex conjunctions between speculations on the subject of desire, interpretive control and the production of poetry engaged more often or more forcefully. Interpretation, authority for narration and erotic activity are inextricably intertwined. The terms which are conjoined in these activities are by no means consistent. Certain texts refuse difference either by the petulant assertion of masculine dominance, or by an idealization of woman. Other poems euphorically affirm multiplicity. The questions which concern us here are not just connected with the opposing terms of sexual "identities," but also with the shifting differences within sexuality. We are led to read Baudelaire's texts less as explorations of the enigma of sex than as explorations of differences which make sex and literature enigmatic.

Perhaps the best known passages in Baudelaire which link sexual difference to artistic production are the petulant and often contradictory assertions in the *Journaux intimes*. A brief and very suggestive discussion of these passages is proposed by Leo Bersani in his book *Baudelaire and Freud*.[4] His consideration of "shifting sexual identities" deals with the dialectic between art and life and its disruption, and with the constitution of the artist's self.[5] One series of passages establishes a homology between love, art and prostitution:

> L'amour, c'est le goût de la prostitution ...
> Qu'est-ce l'art? Prostitution.   (1247)
>
> Qu'est-ce que l'amour?
> Le besoin de sortir de soi.
> L'homme est un animal adorateur.
> Adorer, c'est se sacrifier et se prostituer.
> Aussi tout amour est-il prostitution.

L'être le plus prostitué, c'est l'être par excellence, c'est Dieu, puisqu'il est l'ami suprême pour chaque individu, puisqu'il est le réservoir commun, inépuisable de l'amour.   (1286–7)

Love/prostitution is the need to "go outside oneself." Prostitution is sacred, since the most prostituted being is the supreme being. A second series of quotations deals with appetite, the contrasting relations of masculinity and femininity to desire and the assertion that cultivation of the arts is a masculine activity:

21

La femme a faim et elle veut manger. Soif, et elle veut boire.
Elle est en rut et elle veut être foutue.
Le beau mérite!
La femme est *naturelle*, c'est-à-dire abominable. (1247)

Plus l'homme cultive les arts, moins il bande.
Il se fait un divorce de plus en plus sensible entre l'esprit et la
    brute.
La brute seule bande bien, et la fouterie est le lyrisme du
    peuple.
Foutre, c'est aspirer à entrer dans un autre, et l'artiste ne sort
    jamais de lui-même. (1295–6)

Woman, here, is a metaphor for unconstrained desire, which in
Baudelaire's lexicon is designated as "natural," and is condemned.
Art is a masculine activity which mediates this brutishness; the
artist never goes outside of himself. The first series of quotes,
however, proposes art as a feminine activity; the artist is "open" to
"penetration" by forms alien to him, and his receptivity is both holy
and degrading. An ecstasy-producing shock shatters what Bersani
calls the "self's integrity," in a powerful sexual event: "psychic
penetrability is fantasized as sexual penetrability."[6] Complications
introduced by the second series of pronouncements are interpreted
as signs of Baudelaire's resistance to his own powerful intuitions.
The spiritualization of art, which would contain art within the
bounds of traditional oppositions between activities of the flesh and
the spirit is a "self-protective immobility."[7] Bersani's most powerful insight here is in tracing a dynamics of forces which resist
Baudelaire's most radical practices, and in locating the figural
processes which inscribe these incompatibilities. The loss which
Bersani finds in these texts, however, is the sort of shift which
makes possible a very considerable gain. These texts, in their
tenacious adherence to a series of oppositions which refuse to
remain stable, between masculine/feminine and self/other, suggest
how problematic these terms are and how vulnerable they are to
dysfunction; a complex of contradictions introduces the beginnings
of a radical instability within polarities.

la femme, en un mot, n'est pas seulement pour l'artiste en général, et pour
M. G. en particulier, la femelle de l'homme. C'est plutôt une divinité, un
astre, qui préside à toutes les conceptions du cerveau mâle; c'est un
miroitement de toutes les grâces de la nature condensées dans un seul être;
c'est l'objet de l'admiration et de la curiosité la plus vive que le tableau de
la vie puisse offrir au contemplateur.

("Le Peintre de la Vie moderne," 1181)

The speculations begin with a formula which takes as its point of reference an unquestioned masculine identity. The poet's statement that woman is not just the biological female of man affirms, of course, that she is indeed just that . . . but more. Each characteristic of woman's otherness reaffirms the centrality of the male subject; he is the active source of conception, whose curiosity and high regard interpret woman in terms of his own desire and understanding. Woman presides over a fertile male mind. She is a complex mirror which concentrates and returns the image of nature for the enjoyment of the viewing subject; she is the object of admiration offered to the male observer (*le contemplateur*). This passage attempts to retrieve an enigmatic supplementarity to the controlling interpretation of the subject. The question is not just that of the relation between the sexes, however, for the passage engages the more general problematic of the artist's authority and ability to make sense of the world seen as an orderly construct ("le tableau de la vie"). Woman is not only the object of sexual and spiritual desire, she is the figure for everything in the world that is desirable and knowable.

Turning to a few texts in the prose poems, I would like to trace some of the ways in which a desired unity of a male subject is dislodged, violently shattered or disengaged in a pleasurable affirmation of multiplicity.

The figuration of sexuality which we have been reading resists multiple and partial meanings. The preface to the prose poems, a letter-poem to Arsène Houssaye, on the other hand, celebrates the incomplete, the diverse and the fragmentary. The poet offers the book to the editor and reader as a group of fragments, without implying any underlying nostalgia for a lost or unattainable totality. The interest of this preface is not that it can be read as a metapoetic statement about the book; occupying the position of preface, it places in question the difference between poem and preface, of fulfilled intention and the supremacy of the head. What comes at the head of the book, as Barbara Johnson has remarked, is the absence of head; the preface decapitates the text.[8]

The opening paragraph of the dedication compares the text to the body of a serpent and goes on to enumerate the remarkable properties of a text/beast whose integrity is to be found in a very complex disorder. The body of the text can be cut into fragments and rearranged at will, endlessly:

Mon cher, ami, je vous envoie un petit ouvrage dont on ne pourrait pas dire, sans injustice, qu'il n'a ni queue ni tête, puisque tout, au contraire, y est à la fois tête et queue, alternativement et réciproquement. Considérez, je vous prie, quelles admirables commodités cette combinaison nous offre à tous, à vous, à moi et au lecteur. Nous pouvons couper où nous voulons, moi ma rêverie, vous le manuscrit, le lecteur sa lecture; car je ne suspends pas la volonté rétive de celui-ci au fil interminable d'une intrigue superflue. Enlevez une vertèbre, et les deux morceaux de cette tortueuse fantaisie se rejoindront sans peine. Hachez-la en nombreux fragments, et vous verrez que chacun peut exister à part. Dans l'espérance que quelques-uns de ces tronçons seront assez vivants pour vous plaire et vous amuser, j'ose vous dédier le serpent tout entier. (229)

The figure of the segmented serpent is perhaps less interesting for what it says about the absence of a general narrative line connecting the poems and of sequential order in the collection, than for what it suggests about the disruption of an ideal of totality presumed characteristic of all books. This passage opens up the possibility of extending that disruption to the poem, the writing subject and the narrated object.

Baudelaire states quite explicitly in the passage we have quoted that there is to be found in this text neither an overall thematic structure nor a narrative sequence. The thread of narrative logic has been cut: "je ne suspends pas la volonté rétive de celui-ci [le lecteur] au fil interminable d'une intrigue superflue." The traditional equation between prose and narrative is thus subverted from the outset as far as it would provide an architecture for the poetic structure of the entire text. These disruptions are not insignificant, but they are hardly radical, for although there is no general narrative logic to the collection as a whole, nor a thematic structure, each might itself remain a self-sufficient poetic unit: "Hachez-la en nombreux fragments, et vous verrez que *chacun peut exister à part.*" On one level, then, the passage proposes some rather explicit statements about the collection: the texts can be read as isolated fragments; remove one segment and the series will restore itself to unity in an infinite number of different patterns. At this point, the notion of meaningful closure characteristic of this book as a whole has been questioned, but the passage could easily be read as simply displacing that notion upon the individual text. One critic has even referred to the tight control exercised by the narrator in these well-constructed texts and reproaches them for their "narrative comfort."[9]

I would like to suggest that the figure of the fragmented serpent generates meanings not so easily collected or assimilated as our reading thus far may have intimated. The metaphor of the segmented serpent inscribes the figure here in what might be called a rhetoric of disruption, which operates at the same time a forceful disruption of rhetoric. The energy of that process is suggested by the violent language of this passage, which characterizes composition, editing and reading as acts of cutting, interrupting and displacing fragments: "Nous pouvons couper où nous voulons ... Enlèvez une vertèbre ... Hachez-la en nombreux fragments ... ces tronçons ..." The scattered bits of this metaphor suggest the possibility of a poetic discourse whose meanings would be simultaneously limited and contained and would also be plural, undecidable. The figure asserts both the value of the distinction between proper and figurative (the serpent is not without head or tail) and problematizes that distinction from within by putting in question the hierarchy between the terms on which the distinction is grounded. The order of meaning does not altogether abolish a certain delimitation of sense, in which serpents have heads and tails, it denies and exceeds the possibility of restoring the primacy of those meanings. This figure problematizes the question of difference in ways which always deflect a return to the "conceptions of the male mind," and hierarchical orders such as those in the passages considered earlier.

I would like to turn to three prose poems, "Le Mauvais Vitrier," "Le Vieux Saltimbanque" and "Portraits de Maîtresses." In the first two, the narrator encounters a double; the narcissistic similarity of the other in these poems, threatens the narrator with a death-like immobility ("Le Vieux Saltimbanque") or produces a liberating violence which destroys the specular bond ("Le Mauvais Vitrier"). Without the protective veil of feminine difference, the narrator's relation to specular figures is always sado-masochistically aggressive. The violence of these confrontations enables the narrator to break away from the sado-masochistic bonds. Aggression is neither a will to appropriate nor a perpetuation of an erotic suffering. In one way or another, these confrontations with the double constitute an impasse which the narrator goes about dismantling, even if he does not precisely resolve it. The third poem, "Portraits de Maîtresses," carries to the extreme the impasses we have been considering in a comic exchange of sexual roles which ultimately disrupts generic oppositions from within.

"Le Mauvais Vitrier" begins with some observations about bizarre characters who engage unpredictably in certain impulsive actions:

25

The Limits of narrative

Il y a des natures purement contemplatives et tout à fait impropres à l'action, qui cependant, sous une impulsion mystérieuse et inconnue, agissent quelquefois avec une rapidité dont elles se seraient crues elles-mêmes incapables. (238)

The agent of action in this text is an already deconstructed subject. The mad energy which precipitates these persons toward action exceeds their consciousness in a performance which appears to assert full and calculated control. The fortuitous inspiration which traverses the actor renders questionable the very possibility of the subject:

(Observez, je vous prie, que l'esprit de mystification qui, chez quelques personnes, n'est pas le résultat d'un travail ou d'une combinaison, mais d'une inspiration fortuite, participe beaucoup, ne fût-ce que par l'ardeur de désir, de cette humeur, hystérique selon les médicins, satanique selon ceux qui pensent un peu mieux que les médecins, . . .) (239)

The poet briefly recounts several anecdotes in which indolent dreamers perform absurd and excessive actions. One sets fire to a forest, to see how quickly the fire will spread; another lights a cigar next to a powder keg, to discover the pleasures of anxiety, or perhaps for no reason at all; a third, painfully timid, enthusiastically embraces a stranger on the street. The narrator's own story is similar in its irrationality, but, unlike the others, it functions in important ways in the register of language. The story, then, deals in a crucial way not only with action, but suggests that action and language are inseparable:

Un matin je m'étais levé maussade, triste, fatigué d'oisiveté, et poussé, me semblait-il, à faire quelquechose de grand, *une action d'éclat*; et j'ouvris la fenêtre, hélas! (239, italics added)

Even before the action has been executed, the performance is associated with the figural motif of fragmentation; as a disarticulation of unity (*une action d'éclat*), a splendid act, is brilliantly linked already to the figure of shattering glass.

The anecdote in which the narrator figures as an actor recounts his invitation to an itinerant glazier to climb six flights of stairs to the poet's room to show him his wares. He then shrilly rebukes the merchant for not offering for sale colored glass, rose, red, blue: "des vitres de paradis . . . " The peddler is thrust into the staircase and, as he emerges below, the narrator bombards him with a flower pot which destroys the glazier's entire stock. The narrator then cries out: "La vie en beau! La vie en beau!" This attack is launched

26

by an already deconstructed subject against an allegorical figure of failed idealist art. The smashing act (*une action d'éclat*) produces intense pleasure (*l'infini de la jouissance*) by breaking a specular bond. It also shatters the metaphoric medium (*verre/vers*) of an idealist art, both transparent to "reality" and capable of transforming it. No interpretation of this text should attempt to pick up the pieces by suggesting what alternative there might be to the glazier's stock; what is important is the way in which difference divides the acting "subject" and how a metaphor of idealist art is linked to a narcissistic encounter which is then rejected in an explosion of violent and erotic excess.

The narrator in "Le Vieux Saltimbanque" is confronted with another allegorical double and is very nearly drawn into a death-like immobility as he contemplates an old clown abandoned by the crowd, an allegorical figure of the "vieux poète sans amis, sans famille, sans enfants, dégradé par sa misère et par l'ingratitude publique, et dans la baraque de qui le monde oublieux ne veut plus entrer!" The old clown is a degraded figure of the productive comedians whose art the narrator enjoys in the first part of the poem, as he participates in "L'explosion frénétique de la vitalité." In the first part of the text, before the encounter with the old clown, the narrator strolls among the booths of a carnival where he sees a number of performers; clowns, strong men and dancers. Sound, movement and performance are everywhere:

... je ne manque jamais, en vrai Parisien, de passer la revue de toutes les baraques se pavanent à ces époques solennelles.

Elles se faisaient, en vérité, une concurrence formidable: elles piaill-aient, beuglaient, hurlaient. C'était un mélange de cris, de détonations de cuivre et d'explosions de fusées. Les queues-rouges et les Jocrisses convulsaient les traits de leurs visages basanés, racornis par le vent, la pluie et le soleil; il lançaient, avec l'aplomb des comédiens sûrs de leurs effets, des bons mots et des plaisanteries d'un comique solide et lourd, comme celui de Molière. (247–8)

The fair is a festival which celebrates exchange ("les uns dépen-saient, les autres gagnaient, les uns et les autres également joyeux."), yet it is impossible to say in this equally joyous encounter who spends and who collects. The crowd spends and consumes; the comedians' performance is at once an expenditure of energy and a production of meaning and pleasure. Both the crowd and the actors gain from the other's expense. This passage, then, disrupts a circuit of exchange between the performer and the consumer of meaning. Sense and energy are not transformed into objects which can be appropriated but circulate according to a different economy. Opposed to this vitality is the stillness of the clown: "Il était immobile." This allegorical double of the poet functions in a different register of meaning whose effects are indeed deadening. The reflection of the same threatens the narrator with destruction of voice and sight, which serve here as metonymies for the artist's faculties:

Je sentis ma gorge serrée par la main terrible de l'hystérie, et il me sembla que mes regards étaient offusqués par ces larmes rebelles qui ne veulent pas tomber. (248–9)

The exchange proposed here is a one-way affair, a charitable act which would permit the narrator to escape from the allegorical figure and to return to the vitality of the crowd. The poet resolves to leave a coin on the edge of the clown's stall. By chance, however, the offering is never made and the narrator is swept away by the crowd and thrown back into multiplicity, rescued from a debilitating specularity: "un grand reflux de peuple, causé par je ne sais quel trouble, m'entraîna loin de lui." The poem concludes with an interpretation of the allegorical narrative, the passage quoted in the beginning of this discussion. The text by no means obliterates the allegorical reading, however, in favor of an unproblematic economy of multiplicity. The allegory thematizes an impending death which threatens both the narrator and his double by fixing the effects of meaning. The text sets the stage for the death of this meaning, yet it survives in a curiously problematic manner. The narrator is suspended between two kinds of meaning, located neither in ecstatic multiplicity into which the crowd has thrown him once again, nor in the immobilizing specular duality of the allegory, which retains an enduring and obsessive fascination.[10]

The perfect equivalence between the thoughts and souls of a lover/narrator and his mistress ("rêvé par tous les hommes ... réalisé par aucun ... " "Les Yeux de Pauvres") not only fails as a dream of symmetry, but to the degree that it appears to succeed in "Portraits de Maîtresses," produces monsters, women who assume a monomaniacal "male" consistency. The four narrators of this poem survive the affairs they recount not only by rejecting or being rejected by their mistresses, but by assuming a certain femininity: it is a narration engendered by sexual difference within gender. The poem is introduced as the most banal of subjects, an after-dinner conversation between men about women, yet the first sentence, in the context of the entire narrative, can be read as something more than a cliché. "Dans un boudoir d'hommes, c'est-à-dire, dans un fumoir attenant à un élégant tripot, quatres hommes fumaient et buvaient" (293). The stereotype here, of course, is that men who gossip about women are, as gossips, women. Beyond that commonplace, however, there is an interesting association between narrating and interpreting and men who assume a certain bi-sexuality; the men are not just the female of men, they are at once men and women. In each of the four anecdotes, the break between mistress and lover is occasioned when the woman assumes an oddly "masculine" consistency. The disequilibrium of differences which activates sexuality, and proliferates supplementary meaning, has been stilled by an obsessive continuity.

The first narrator prefaces his story by characterizing four cycles of love, the final stage being the absence of desire, "le calme absolu," which we can assume will never produce narrative. Having passed through "l'âge de Chérubin ... où, faute de dryades, on embrasse le tronc des chênes," and a second stage which is the beginning of decadence, as one begins to choose, the narrator has arrived at a third and rather sexually ambiguous cycle of love: "l'époque climatérique du troisième degré où la beauté ne suffit plus, si elle n'est assaisonnée par le parfum, la parure, et cetera." Desire is provoked not by what is stated to be *proper* to woman, beauty, but by what supplements it; little matter what is supplied, it is otherness which counts (*et cetera*).

The first speaker's mistress was: "une femme qui voulait toujours faire l'homme. 'Vous n'êtes pas un homme! Ah! si j'étais un homme! De nous deux, c'est moi que suis l'homme!' " (294). One day she takes up chemistry and it is only when he finds his Minerva ("affamée de force idéale") in a compromising situation with his domestic that he is moved to turn her out.[11]

The second narrator's mistress, "la plus douce, la plus soumise et la plus dévouée des créatures," though always ready for his passion, is frigid. He tires of this "duel inégal," in which, we may assume, he is always vanquished. She marries another man, has six children and later confesses to the narrator that "l'épouse est encore aussi *vierge* que ne l'était votre maîtresse." In a sense, as the intact, virgin mother she has remained consistent to a phobic male ideal, which the second narrator implicitly recognizes.[12]

The third mistress was always hungry; she is a figure of woman as unconstrained appetite, such as we encountered earlier, but with a difference. She ends up with an employee of the quartermaster corps: "que fournit peut-être à cette pauvre enfant la ration de plusieurs soldats" (295). Her appetite has made of her not just a monster (*"monstre polyphage"*) but a soldier.

The fourth and longest story is told by a rather severe narrator, whose appearance is almost clerical; he is uncompromising, unforgiving. His mistress's defect was her excessive virtue, which constantly improved upon his own moral rectitude. He characterizes her as "le contraire de ce que l'on reproche à l'égoiste femelle" (295). This "contrary" woman becomes, in fact, the specular figure of the narrator:

> Figurez-vous une personne incapable de commettre une erreur de sentiment ou de calcul; figurez-vous une sérénité désolante de caractère; un dévouement sans comédie et sans emphase; une douceur sans faiblesse; . . .
> (296)

A series of figures characterizes her in terms of a specular relation to the narrator; their love "ressemble à un interminable voyage sur une surface pure et polie comme un miroir, vertigineusement monotone, qui aurait réfléchi tous mes sentiments et mes gestes avec l'exactitude ironique de ma propre conscience . . . " (296). She is his inseparable spectre:

> je ne pouvais pas me permettre un geste ou un sentiment déraisonnable sans apercevoir immédiatement le reproche muet de *mon inséparable spectre* (296, italics added)

Finally, the violence internalized by this super-super-ego threatens to destroy the narrator; instead:

> Un soir, dans un bois . . . au bord d'une mare . . . après une mélancholique promenade où ses yeux, à elle, réfléchissaient la douceur du ciel, et où mon coeur, à moi, était crispé comme l'enfer . . .
> – Quoi!
> – Comment!
> – Que voulez-vous dire?
> – C'était inévitable. (296–7)

The encounter with difference conceived in terms of an ideal of unity, in its positive or negative versions, creates violence and victims in "Le Mauvais Vitrier" and "Portraits de Maîtresses." The destructive ideal of a perfect union of thought and sentiment produces a very significant misreading by the narrator in "Les Yeux des Pauvres." In that poem the poet addresses the narrative to his mistress as an example of her impenetrability: "vous êtes, je crois,

30

le plus bel exemple d'imperméabilité féminine qui se puisse rencontrer" (268). It is a mock-serious story in which the narrator not only chides his mistress for her insensitivity but also takes an ironic attitude toward his own feelings of remorse. The meaning of the text, however, is not played out exclusively in an ethical register. The poem has much to do with the availability of meaning in the various eyes described in the course of the narrative, and we learn that meaning cannot be in the I of the observer.

The disabused narrator advances his own desire for a union of thought and sentiment between lover and mistress as an unoriginal, though persistent dream of all *men*:

Nous avions passé ensemble une longue journée qui m'avait paru courte. Nous nous étions bien promis que toutes nos pensées nous seraient communes à l'un et à l'autre, et que nos deux âmes désormais n'en feraient plus qu'une; – un rêve qui n'a rien d'original, après tout, si ce n'est que, rêvé par tous les hommes, il n'a été réalisé par aucun.   (268)

We know from the opening lines of the text, quoted above, that the story purports to illustrate the futility of this dream, yet it also says much about the impasses produced by the desire for a certain kind of access to meaning and about the disruptions of the opposition between impenetrable (illegible) and penetrable (readable) meanings. The poem recounts a pathetic scene in which a destitute father and his two children gaze from the sidewalk in astonishment at the narrator and his mistress inside a sumptuous café. Each of the three gazes "speaks" to the poet; he reads in their eyes a message which he "quotes" to his mistress in reported speech. It is as though he finds a perfect equivalence between a readable surface and an expressive voice. The father of this bedraggled group marvels at the rich gold which adorns the walls of the café. The first child repeats his father's exclamations ("que c'est beau! que c'est beau!") and observes that only people who are not like them may enter. Only a stupid joy can be read in the second child's eyes.

The sequence is an example of a "perfect communication" in which interpretation reads meaning and gives it voice seemingly without difference or loss. This legibility gives rise to the charitable guilt of a good conscience:

Non seulement j'étais attendri par cette famille d'yeux, mais je me sentais un peu honteux de nos verres et de nos carafes, plus grands que notre soif.   (269)

The narrator leans toward his mistress to affirm his own reading:

31

Je tournais mes regards vers les vôtres, cher amour, pour y lire *ma* pensée; je plongeais dans vos yeux si beaux et si bizarrement doux, dans vous yeux verts, habités par le Caprice et inspiré par la Lune,... (269)

It may be suspected that there is more to read here than the narrator's reproaches would suggest. Is the poem simply an ironic moral tale about feminine capriciousness and insensitivity? The woman in this passage is quite traditionally the locus of unstable sense, capriciousness, which the narrator desires to fill with a reflection of his own thought. Not only does she not provide the desired intelligible surface which can be penetrated by interpretation, she deflects the interpretation by returning her gaze and the narrator's attention to the pauper's eyes. There she reads ... nothing, or so it would seem:

"Ces gens-là me sont insupportables avec leurs yeux ouverts comme des portes cochères! ..." (269)

In a sense this gesture simply repeats that of the narrator earlier in the text, but there are crucial differences. The woman has not read a fully meaningful literal message such as the poet had found, but she has not really discovered the obverse of that sense: an absence of meaning. She does not find a "proper" sense, but a simile ("*comme* des portes cochères"), which figures a gaping place of passage. Although this reading is presented as evidence of an irritating lack of sensitivity on the part of this mistress and opposed implicitly by the narrator's assumed sympathy for the poor, the ethical message can be considered as a strategy to limit our reading to the narrator's interpretation. Links between the poet's "charity" and a narcissistic appropriation of difference are obscured. The narrator's regard seeks to read its own thought in a sure duplication of the self. What is produced, however, is not a reflexive process, but what we might call a "deflexive" process, a different reading of the other which is figuratively open to any and all meaning. The woman does not stop meaning; she short-circuits a certain kind of meaning.

The text concludes with an ironic complaint about the difficulties of understanding and loving:

Tant il est difficile de s'entendre, mon cher ange, et tant la pensée, est incommunicable, même entre gens qui s'aiment! (269)

This statement repeats, of course, the explicit point of departure, for this reflection on reflexivity demystifies communion, and not incidentally an ethic to which it is linked. When the woman short-circuits the projection and exchange of meanings, she introduces an inscription to which this narrator is blind. She poses the problem of readability in a very different way and sets radically different terms for the interpretive act by deflecting the ultimately narcissistic desire for communication. The woman's action suggests that the space of meaning cannot be appropriated as the proper, but must always be read as a figure which is located elsewhere from the space one desires.

Relations of difference in the poem "Le Thyrse" are initially set in an equilibrium within duality. Two series interact; a masculine series, which is associated with the single stick which is said to serve as the center and organizing force of the caduseus, and a feminine series, the flowers and vines which are entwined about the stick.

> Qu'est-ce qu'un thyrse? Selon le sens moral et poétique, c'est un emblème sacerdotal dans la main des prêtres et des prêtresses célébrant la divinité dont ils sont les interprètes et les serviteurs. Mais physiquement ce n'est qu'un bâton, un pur bâton, perche à houblon, tuteur de vigne, sec, dur et droit. Autour de ce bâton, dans des méandres capricieux, se jouent et folâterent des tiges et des fleurs, celles-ci sinueuses et fuyardes, celles-là penchées comme des cloches ou des coupes renversées.   (285)

The opposition between masculine and feminine elements in this "astonishing duality," which is implicit in the above passage, is elaborated in more explicit detail:

> Le bâton, c'est votre volonté, droite, ferme et inébranlable, les fleurs, c'est la promenade de votre fantaisie autour de votre volonté; c'est l'élément féminin exécutant autour du mâle ses prestigieuses pirouettes. Ligne droite et ligne arabesque, intention et expression, roideur de la volonté, sinuosité du verbe, unité du but, variété des moyens.   (285)

Duality, however, is neither the simple opposition between figural and literal meanings advanced by the first definition, nor the oppositions between masculine and feminine metaphorized in the second passage. Binary order is already problematized in the first passage by the drift away from metaphoric, emblematic sense into a literal meaning. In the second passage, what is assumed to be most proper, sexual difference, is described as an interplay of metaphors. Difference here, as Barbara Johnson has written, is not limited to binary relations between terms in equilibrium, but is played out as a complex entanglement of relations, in which no term is ever proper without being at the same time figurative.[13]

The poem is dedicated to the musician Franz Liszt and ends with a lyrical apostrophe to the musician, but the sexual gender signified by the pronoun *vous* in that passage is curiously unstable. The narrator speaks of the astonishing duality of the "maître puissant et vénéré," and, in the same context, addresses an apostrophe to the "cher Bacchant de la Beauté." The text thus presents in a grammatically masculine form a term which normally occurs in the feminine: *Bacchante*, a priestess of Bacchus. Furthermore "his" art is said to be equal to that of the frenzied nymphs of Bacchus. Identity of this genius is established by sexual reversal, which is then supplemented by another reversal:

Jamais nymphe exaspérée par l'invincible Bacchus ne secoua son thryse sur les têtes de ses compagnons affolées avec autant d'énergie et de caprice que vous agitez votre génie sur les coeurs de vos frères.   (285)

Beyond this undecidable sexual ambiguity, the subject *vous* is constituted as an interaction of masculine and feminine terms, which are themselves figures.

Before the passages we have just read, the narrator enjoins the reader, and himself as well, from establishing a hierarchy of value among terms:

qui osera décider si les fleurs et les pampres ont été fait pour le bâton, ou si le baton n'est que le prétexte pour montrer la beauté des pampres et des fleurs?   (285)

The conclusion to that paragraph repeats the injunction against analyzing, separating the "amalgame tout-puissant et indivisible du génie." The "indivisible," however, is a complex of difference. The distinctions between proper and figural and those between masculine and feminine on which a stable definition of the subject might rest remain undecidable, and circulate as shifting elements of difference. It is that circulation in "Le Thyrse," rather than a balance within duality, which generates an intricate network of meaning and interpretation, and produces, beyond a tension within equilibrium, both intense pleasure and anguish (*Volupté*, *Angoisse*).

What characterizes a modern existence, we recall from the preface to the prose poems, is not just that it is lived *in* a modern city, but that "frequenting" great cities is experienced as a "criss-crossing of their innumerable relations" ("le croisement de leurs innombrales rapports" 229). The viewing, narrating, interpreting subject, then, is not defined by its relation to totality or a center, but by multiple links to plurality which is visited, celebrated again and again (*fréquenter*). The sense of the city and of the interpreting "subject" is produced by these intersections of multiple relations.[14] Three poems, "Les Fenêtres," "Les Projets," and "Les Foules," are particularly interesting for the ways in which they engage criss-crossings of multiplicity in their accounts of desire and poetic invention.

In "Les Fenêtres," the experience of knowing one's being and what one is ("sentir que je suis et ce que je suis") results from a curious indifference to sexual identity and to any stable identity of the objects of desire. The other upon whose story the narrator builds his own sense of identity becomes simply a variable mark of difference. The poet proposes to know himself through the interpretation of the object he observes; an old woman, bent over her work, whom he sees through a window. This figure, however, becomes just that ... a figure, a series of multiple metonyms, fragments of a non-existent totality.

The closed, yet transparent window and the frame in which it is set would appear to establish the descriptive coordinates for an ideal transfer of meaning; the window appears to serve as a metaphor for the transparent sense, which is accessible beyond a signifying surface as a deeper, internal signified.[15]

Celui qui regarde du dehors à travers une fenêtre ouverte, ne voit jamais autant de choses que celui qui regarde une fenêtre fermée.   (288)

The metaphoric sense of the window prepares us to accept that no surface is opaque to the penetrating gaze of the observer. The scene viewed through the transparent glass, we suppose will yield its inner, deeper secrets, just as readily as the glass facilitates the passage of the interpreting gaze. The window, while seeming to justify the possibility of literal meaning, itself functions as a metaphor of literality. The supposed "naturalness" of this operation is neither "innocent" of figuration nor uncomplex; the vehicle of literal meaning is a metaphor which provides access to a surface, the body of the woman, which itself produces a series of metonyms.

Avec son visage, avec son vêtement, avec son geste, avec presque rien, j'ai refait l'histoire de cette femme, ou plutôt sa légende, et quelquefois je me la raconte à moi-même en pleurant.   (288)

This distinction between *histoire* and *légende* is similar to that between the whole woman and the metonymic fragments: what counts is not a true and total sense, but the operations which produce fiction. The term *légende* in its opposition to *histoire* sets fiction over and against *truth*. Meaning, here, does not inhere to the meaningful object of attention to be retrieved by the narrator as a past; it is a fiction produced by a fragmented surface as "what is read" (*légende*). It is not a question here of the literal nor of truth, but of desire, interpretation and telling ("et quelquefois, je me la raconte à moi-même en pleurant").

As the narration continues, indifference to identity is even more radical than it first appeared:

Si c'eût été un pauvre vieux homme, j'aurais refait la sienne tout aussi aisément.   (288)

Either man or woman, the figure functions as the signifier of the availability of meaning.

The conclusion to the text responds to a question posed by a hypothetical reader and raises explicitly the issue of the truth of the narrator's stories:

Peut-être me direz-vous: "Es-tu sûr que cette légende soit la vraie?" Qu'importe ce que peut-être la réalité placée hors de moi, si elle n'a aidée à vivre, à sentir que je suis et ce que je suis?   (288)

The substitution of an individual truth for a universal truth would seem to indicate that our reading of the text is mystified; the poet has simply imposed singular, personal meaning instead of a generalized, universal sense, just as he had earlier substituted legend for history. *Being* the self, possessing an internalized "reality," however, results from living by means of a fiction indifferent to truth and generated by figures lacking ontological substance. The poet "exists" then, only through the stories of desire; a "true legend" is one which constitutes the "subject" as multiple effects of signifiers. Throughout the poem the metaphoric resonances of the associations produced by frame, transparent surface and depth, which would seem to limit and provide access to a central meaning are countered forcefully by the interplay of metonym, fragment and difference.

Similar disruptions are produced by framed scenes in "Les Projets." The narrator's itinerary in his poem links four different spaces; a public park, a street, a large avenue, and his own apartment: each decor generates a series of signifiers from which the narrator constructs a dream of future bliss with his mistress. While each space frames a scene into which the narrator projects a narrative of future erotic pleasure and sentimental communication, it is the multiplicity of the desiring subject and the changes of his mistress which keep desire and interpretation alive. In the first sequence, the narrator imagines his companion as a princess:

36

"Comme elle serait belle dans un costume de cour, compliqué et fastueux, descendent, à travers l'atmosphère d'un beau soir, les degrés de marbre d'un palais, en face des grandes pelouses et des bassins! Car elle a naturellement l'air d'une princesse." (265)

In a second fantasy, an engraving seen in a shop window provides the pretext for reverie. Rejecting the palace as the ideal place to "possess her dear life" the narrator turns toward the details of the engraving:

"Au bord de la mer, une belle case en bois, enveloppée de tous ces arbres bizarres et luisants dont j'ai oublié les noms . . . , dans l'atmosphère une odeur enivrante, indéfinissable . . . , dans la case un puissant parfum de rose et du musc . . . , plus loin, derrière notre petit domaine, des bouts de mâts balancés par la houle . . . , autour de nous, au delà la chambre . . . "
(265)

As in the preceding passage, desire is produced not just by the mistress herself, but by metonymic supplements, costume or decor.[16] Here the description moves from fragment to fragment; it is not only the significance of the detail which produces pleasure, but the mobility of the interpreting imagination, constantly in movement. The profusion of detail and the use of deletion marks in this poem suggest the possibility of a potentially limitless expansion of the scene. It is not just the narrator's affective affinity with the decor which excites his imagination, but the generative power of language which shows itself so clearly in this passage. There is always the suggestion that the space of lack exists only to be filled by description, yet that space is the sign of the possibility of meaning which is there in the details of the description and ever lacking (. . .); the space is an invitation to pleasure.[17]

The third decor, by contrast with the first two, is domestic, familiar and bourgeois, yet equally powerful in its capacity to figure the possibility of enjoyment:

il aperçut une auberge proprette, où d'une fenêtre égayée par des rideaux d'indienne bariolée se penchaient deux têtes rieuses. (265–6)

Reproaching his imagination for its vagaries, the narrator once again corrects his fantasy:

Le plaisir et le bonheur sont dans la première auberge venue, dans l'auberge du hasard, si féconde en voluptés. (266)

The last scene is set in the poet's apartment, an interior which invites untroubled reflection:

Et en rentrant seul chez lui, à cette heure où les conseils de la Sagesse ne sont plus étouffés par les bourdonnements de la vie extérieure.... (266)

This conclusion is framed by a symbolically enclosed space and presented under the tutelage of an allegorical Figure of Wisdom, but like the three preceding scenes, it does not establish closure of meaning. It is neither the final scene in the series which the narrative has opened up, nor the moment in which private imagination abandons the fantasies of earlier scenes to take pleasure in a present enjoyment finally possessed. The conclusion opens up on a limitless journey of the imagination:

"J'ai eu aujourd'hui, en rêve, trois domiciles où j'ai trouvé un égal plaisir. Pourquoi contraindre mon corps à changer de place, puisque mon âme voyage si lestement? Et à quoi bon exécuter des projets, puisque le projet est en lui-même une jouissance suffisante?" (1660)

Enjoyment is always a *project*, located elsewhere, completing, or rather supplementing the woman, set in a future, hypothetical moment. Satisfaction is projected as the proliferation of infinitely different scenes of desire, each *equal* to the other as a possibility, yet part of an open series which defers indefinitely the desired "possession" of the other. As in "Les Fenêtres," otherness and multiplicity form the desiring subject; there is neither a single object of desire nor a unique desiring subject. Both the masculine and feminine figures are plural, always already elsewhere. The project is movement and interpretation.

In "Les Foules" the object of desire is even more plural than in "Les Fenêtres" and "Les Projets"; it is a multiform humanity in which the poet immerses himself ("un bain de multitude" 243). The crowd is characterized by its availability to an active, conventionally "masculine" poet ("le poète actif et fécond" 243), yet the crowd also assumes a traditionally "masculine," active role as it penetrates the poet's consciousness. In giving of himself in an act of "holy prostitution," the poet is also a woman: "cette sainte prostitution de l'âme qui se donne toute entière, poésie et charité, à l'imprévu qui se montre, à l'inconnu qui passe" (244). There is a familiar conjunction here between words which designate being, artistic activity and sexual enjoyment, which links these terms according to conventionally masculine (active) and feminine (passive) roles:

jouir de la foule est un art ... celui-là seul peut faire ... une ribote de vitalité ... La poète jouit de cette incomparable privilège, qu'il peut à sa guise être lui-même et autrui ... Le promeneur solitaire et pensif tire une singulière ivresse de cette universelle communion. ... Celui qui épouse facilement la foule connaît des jouissances fièvreuses ... (243–4)

On certain relations

While they seem firmly in place, terms which characterize subjective communication ("cette universelle communion"), those which designate active and passive roles in knowing, desiring and enjoying and others which designate presence or absence are in fact set adrift from their presumed proper sense. The circuit of communication is supplemented by a mobile network of sense; activity and passivity are reversible, or combine in indeterminate and unstable configurations.

The narrator of "Les Foules" ("le promeneur solitaire et pensif") describes his immersion in the crowd in an idealist lexicon whose central terms occur near the middle of the text: *cette universelle communion*. The activities which are subsumed by this expression, however, are described throughout the text as disruptions of the polarities between the subject and object in a constant exchange and affirmation of differences, without loss or gain of presence. Taking pleasure in the crowd is a performance, analogous to that which the poet enacts in fiction:

jouir de la foule est un art; et celui-là seul peut faire, au dépens du genre humain, une ribote de vitalité, à qui une fée a insufflé dans son berceau le goût du travestissement et du masque, la haine du domicile et la passion du voyage. (243)

This pleasure is accessible through disguise; the mask, the taste for costumes and the passion for travelling serve as figures for the desire to escape self-identity and the definitions imposed by a confining domestic space. Every "self" is a provisional and fleeting project. The poet can be alone in the crowd or can people his solitude, seemingly creating or controlling consciousness at will, but this is possible only when singularity and multiplicity cease to designate separate and distinct states. Solitude is always multiple; one term may generate another in an interplay of difference:

Multitude, solitude: termes égaux et convertibles pour le poète actif et fécond. Qui ne sait pas peupler sa solitude, ne sait pas non plus être seul dans une foule affairée. (243–4)

Possession of others in their meaningful subjectivity, paradoxically, is possible only as the poet becomes indifferent to being:

Il adopte comme siennes toutes les professions, toutes les joies et toutes les misères que la circonstance lui présente.
    Ce que les hommes nomment amour est bien petit, bien restreint et bien faible, comparé à cette ineffable orgie, à cette sainte prostitution de l'âme qui se donne tout entière, poésie et charité, à l'imprévu qui se montre, à l'inconnu qui passe. (244)

39

"Les Foules' is about those libidinal exchanges which disrupt opposition. The "virile" poet is active and fertile, he enters where he will, everything is empty for him. "Prostitute," he gives himself up entirely to the unexpected. What is so striking about the sexual metaphorics of the text is not just that the "virile" artist takes on a "feminine" role, but that both roles are performed alternatively as fictional transformations which destabilize polarized metaphors.

The poem ends with a moral addressed to the contented of this world; the narrator proposes examples of happiness (*des bonheurs*) which surpass their own. Each of the figures celebrated here is a celibate male who knows mysterious pleasures and who has fathered a vast family:

Les fondateurs de colonies, les pasteurs de peuples, les prêtres missionnaires exilés au bout du monde, connaissent sans doute quelque chose de ces mystérieuses ivresses; et, au sein de la vaste famille que leur génie s'est faite, ils doivent rire quelquefois de ceux qui les plaignent pour leur fortune si agitée et pour leur vie si chaste.   (244)

The term *mystérieuses ivresses* links these men's genius to the generative powers of the poet and extends sexual/artistic productivity beyond the disrupted polarities of masculine and feminine activities to include the neuter. The chaste, sexually neuter men become "fertile" through the exercise of their active, fecundating genius. The terms of artistic and sexual identity may appear to remain intact in this passage, however, and even to reinforce paradoxically those which occur throughout the poem; the fertility of the celibate genius would be no different from that of the male artist, who would retrieve in the other a production of himself. The text makes it quite apparent that this schema has a certain basis in power and ideology ("les fondateurs de colonies," "les pasteurs de peuples"), yet this writing has already dislodged the hierarchies upon which that power depends. What would conventionally function as an unmarked term, excluded by the binary opposition between masculine/feminine, has become valorized as yet another mark of difference. Pleasure and meaning are produced in this poem, then, through disruptions of traditionally delimited roles, which here become instances in a mobile and exhilarating network of differences. Is the only laughter at the end of "Les Foules" the moralist's mocking derision directed against the *contented* of this world, or is there perhaps not another kind of outburst, the kind that just will not be contained?

3

EMMA'S STORIES: NARRATIVE, REPETITION AND DESIRE IN *MADAME BOVARY*

– Eh bien! reprit Homais, il faudrait en faire une analyse.
  Car il savait qu'il faut, dans tous les empoisonnements, faire une analyse . . .   (295)

Qu'on n'accuse personne.   (294)[1]

Flaubert's use of narrative in *Madame Bovary* demystifies in many ways the desires which motivate Emma's stories, her fantasies, dreams and her extended fictions of escape and romantic love. Emma's narratives, her protonarratives (fantasies and dreams), her letters to her lovers, the account of her financial ruin told to Lheureux, Binet, Rodolphe and others in the last desperate moments of her life, can be read as repeated and unsuccessful attempts to give order to desires which are destabilizing in their effects and ultimately unattainable. Emma's narratives of desire presuppose closure, bringing on, paradoxically, the death of desire, which cannot live on images of fulfillment, but only on displacements and deferrals.

The division between language and experience is a major concern of the novel. Emma's stories oppose the events which constitute her world, yet lack the force to transform that world. One can attribute Emma's difficulties throughout the novel, then, not just to her foolishness and to the mediocrity of her milieu (although Flaubert clearly treats ironically the shop-worn topos of provincial adultery) but to the more general problems of desire and its realization, and of language and illusion.

Throughout the novel desire, narrative and writing in general produce corrosive effects. These are figured most directly and powerfully, perhaps, during Emma's agony, with the likening of the taste of poison to the taste of ink, and later in the same sequence when the narrator describes a certain black fluid oozing from Emma's mouth. Only a very limited reading, however, would link Emma's desires and her narratives unequivocally to an

41

ultimately mortal alienation of the desiring subject and to writing as death. However demystifying its narrative, the novel *is* a story about desire, with "characters," organized with extraordinary control at certain points of the text by a narrator whose production of fiction must necessarily be interpreted not only as a denial but also a repetition of Emma's relations to narrative and . . . to desire. Once again, what are the possible meanings of that famous statement which Flaubert may or may not have made "Madame Bovary. C'est moi"?

While this chapter focuses on the context and the order of Emma's narratives, it will also re-examine the general problematic of writing in the novel, in the hope that the subject of Emma's narratives will implicate the performance of narrative in the novel itself and, ultimately, the performance of the critical text as well. If Emma is a figure for the writer at a certain point in the history of the novel, this figure does not function exclusively as an uncomplex emblem of the deluded Romantic in an already post-Romantic moment.[2] It may be suspected that the demystification of Emma's narratives does not in fact validate without reserve the control of an enlightened narrator whose understanding transcends the dilemmas of Romantic subjectivity and Romantic literary stereotypes. In many ways, of course, that control is exercised with remarkable force, yet an omniscient narrator is caught in an intricate web of repetition and difference which includes and radically exceeds the logic of identification between narrator and protagonist; includes and exceeds a simple demystification which would deny altogether the links between protagonist and narrator.

An omniscient narrator in *Madame Bovary* is only one among several figures through which narrative is articulated. One of the most fascinating aspects of the novel is the dispersal and fragmentation of authority for narrative. As Barthes has noted, it is impossible to establish with certainty in any comprehensive sense "who speaks" as narrator in this text or from what "point of view."[3] Point of view in *Madame Bovary* can be characterized only by its instability and indeterminacy. It alternates between an omniscient narrator, who knows the motivations of all the protagonists and the truths of the world in which they are placed; a limited point of view, circumscribed by the thoughts and feelings of a particular protagonist; and the even more limited scope of certain minor figures in the text, spectators who have no immediate connection with the major protagonists. The frequent use of free indirect discourse, with its blurring of distinctions between reported speech and narrative, is another complex amalgam of narrative authority.[4] The resulting indeterminacy of point of view, as Culler has demonstrated, is one of the major features of the novel.[5] Those passages which organize narrative according to one or another point of view are countered by others which function in a very different way. The "impersonality" of Flaubert's text, then, is not a distanced objectivity, but a mix of modes of presentation which prevent the reader from identifying a consistent pattern or, to use Rousset's term, modulation. Objectivity is not the absence of narrative authority but a dispersal of that authority which makes it ultimately resistant to recuperative interpretation.

This chapter will question how authority for narrative, both the story of the novel, and Emma's stories framed by the main narrative, is assumed and at the same time problematized. An examination of the composition of Emma's narratives elucidates the ways in which those narratives ironically construct the subject as radically different from what she would be. My assumption is that both narrative form, as well as the stereotypes of narrative content, are necessary to the assertion of desire and intimately related to its failures. The dissolution of the protagonist will be interpreted through perceptible shifts in her relations both to the fictions of desire, the narrative *énoncé*, and to narrative form, both *énoncé* and *énonciation*, as means of ordering and appropriating objects of desire. Finally I will ask how the account and the interpretation of Emma's narratives implicate at once narrators and the reader, as producers of stories: the narratives of desire and the allegories of interpretation.

In a broad sense, *Madame Bovary* gives considerable attention to questions of reading and writing; it narrativizes the interpretation of narrative. The effects of narrative are never merely limited to an explicit content, a subject's relation to the objects of desire, but always open up the more troublesome problematic of how narratives attempt to organize and control desire, how they interpret and construct "reality" and the desiring subject.[6] The power of narrative ordering as a means to fulfil desire and attain knowledge is a ubiquitous motif in this novel. That power fails consistently, as I have suggested, for the effects of fiction-making are quite different from those projected by the desiring subject.

The very control which encourages metanarrative commentary is itself problematized, as in the opening pages of the second part of the novel, when a statement, rare for its explicitness, speaks of the aporia of fictions. The comment serves as a sweeping demystification, yet it doesn't simply write off narrative, for it is set in a transition between the first and second parts of the novel and serves as a preface to a major section of the story. Following a realistic description of the countryside and the village of Yonville, just prior to Charles's and Emma's arrival at their new home, the narrator states simply:

Depuis les événements que l'on va raconter, rien, en effet, n'a changé à Yonville. La drapeau tricolore de fer blanc tourne toujours au haut du clocher de l'église; la boutique du marchand de nouveautés agite encore au vent ses deux banderoles d'indienne; les foetus du pharmacien, comme des paquets d'amadou blanc, se pourrissent de plus en plus dans leur alcool bourbeux, et, au-dessus de la grande porte de l'auberge, le vieux lion d'or, déteint par les pluies, montre toujours aux passants sa frisure de caniche.

(68)

There is a curious complex of meanings here, the sort which will interest me throughout this study. First, a narrator announces in a traditional manner that a new story sequence is about to be related. In an equally traditional fashion, the statement is proleptic; it alludes to the conclusion of the story, known to an omniscient narrator who will relate it to the reader. A moment "beyond narrative" is also posited here, when the main story will have been told and events will return to a meaningless repetition of the same (*toujours, encore*). Narrative, according to this passage, seems to be invested with a significance which is superior to "reality." The world of Yonville after the story, "outside" of narrative, is set against narrative as an endless and seemingly meaningless repetition, which is figured by random motion, the weather vane turning in place, the pennants flapping in the wind, and by the degeneration of the bottled foetuses.

One can also interpret the first sentence of the passage in a very different way, however, as signifying something like: "Events occur, nothing changes." The narrative signified would then be undercut as ultimately insignificant. Thus read, this passage denies the closure of the story about to be told even before it is narrated, as it sets these events against an insignificant post-narrative "reality." While establishing demarcations between story and non-story, the comment problematizes the meaningful difference produced by narrative. I have said that the passage serves as a preface to a section of the novel, and at the same time suggests much about the inconsequentiality of the story; things are further complicated, however, because this is not the *beginning* of the story, but the opening of the second of three major sequences.

Whatever is being said about stories in general must be applied retrospectively to the first part of the novel. The commentary which seems to set itself outside of the main narrative is already framed by the earlier narrative, which can be read as a *commentary* on the metanarrative statement. What is at issue here is less the knowing control over the story by an omniscient narrator who demystifies the fiction from a privileged position, than the impossibility of narrating and at the same time placing oneself outside of the rhetorical operations of fiction. The passage thus becomes engaged in a crisis of narrative whose terms it reiterates in an inevitable play of repetition.[7]

I have already hinted at some of my conclusions about the operations of desire, narrative and interpretation, which can be ordered tentatively in terms of the two statements quoted at the beginning of this chapter. Both quotations are taken from the last pages of the novel. The first is uttered by Homais, panicked when he discovers that Emma has taken poison: "Eh bien! reprit Homais, il faudrait en faire l'analyse. Car il savait qu'il faut, dans tous les empoisonnements, faire une analyse; . . ." (295). In this moment of crisis, the pharmacist unhesitatingly turns toward his science to determine what action must be taken to save Emma from herself. Rapidly moving events prevent Homais from performing his diagnosis, but the critic faced with unsettling problems of interpretation is not subject to such constraints. If we are to analyze the reasons for Emma's destruction in terms of the workings of narrative and accept the guidance of an ironically illusive and sophisticated narrator, we must also accept the tutelage of the pharmacist, that other patron of the analytic process. The imperative to analyze and to achieve interpretive validity allies us unwittingly, yet unfailingly, with Homais.

The other statement informing my reading is a fragment of Emma's suicide letter, which Charles has torn open as Emma lies convulsed on her bed: "*Qu'on n'accuse personne . . .*" (294). At the very moment when it becomes a most urgent concern, we are told in a curiously ambiguous fashion that interpretation is to be suspended. In what ways does Emma's statement serve as an antidote to Homais's disastrously inadequate imperative to undertake analysis? What, in fact, are we being asked not to evaluate? the immediate responsibility for Emma's death? her adultery? or perhaps in a more sweeping sense, those wider issues I have raised – the destructive effects of Emma's relations to fiction? This imperative regarding interpretation, however, is literally suspended, broken by deletion marks in the text. I will return later to the interpretive space opened up by those marks, but let us note for the moment that Homais's and Emma's statements, taken together, point to radically different and incompatible positions concerning the finality of fiction and the necessity for interpretation.[8] The first aims at masterly control and is killing in its effects; the second invites the suspension of judgment and is powerfully productive of interpretation. Inevitably, the reader is engaged by these two imperatives, simultaneously; interpretation circulates between Homais's inept, but nonetheless murderous authority, and Emma's call for the suspension of interpretation.

Learning narrative: a story of one's own

The first part of the novel establishes certain constants in Emma's relation to her desires and the law of the father, which will be repeated throughout the text, and through reiteration, modified. From the outset, Emma's desires are articulated within another's story: paradoxically "her" story is explicitly spoken or already composed by another. In its simplest form, she is the silent and passive object of the story of another's desire, the alienated object of masculine appropriation.

Some of the major preoccupations of the text concerning language and desire, that language is always inadequate to desire, that the language of desire is never unique, but always a common and alienating discourse, are figured early in the novel by the account of Charles's stammering attempts to ask for Emma's hand. This passage marks Emma's entry into the discourse of desire. It is paralleled, as we shall see, by an extensive sequence at the end of the novel which explicitly links the economy of romantic desire with the economy of bourgeois capitalism, when Emma tells the story of her ruin to the men who directly or indirectly contributed to its design. In Part One of the novel Emma undergoes what might be called an apprenticeship to narrative, in which she acquires an individual "voice" for her desires and elaborates them in narrative fictions. Although this section ends with the classic impasse of feminine desire, the "silence" of hysteria, Emma emerges in Part One from the position of a passive voiceless object of desire, to an active fiction making "subject." She theorizes about love, passion and happiness, and composes stories of fulfilled desire. There is an earlier pre-narrative moment, however, which informs all of Emma's subsequent relations to narratives

46

and to desire. Charles attempts to tell Emma's father of his wish to marry her:

> Maître Rouault, murmura-t-il, je voudrais bien vous dire quelque chose.
> Ils s'arrêtèrent. Charles se taisait.
> – *Mais contez-moi votre histoire*! Est-ce que je ne sais pas tout! dit le père Rouault, en riant doucement. (23, italics added)

The formulation of desire here, early in the text, is associated significantly with the ability to compose a story. Charles, of course, has difficulty with stories throughout the novel, and that is part of the reason why his demand is relayed to Emma by her father. There are further implications of this episode, however, which are worth exploring. Throughout the novel Charles will remain deprived of the status of acting subject in the stories of desire. In terms of Emma's stories, he is the silent institutionalized opponent. There is more at issue, however, than Charles's silence and his ultimate exclusion from the stories of desire. Here the figure of the prospective husband and that of the father are conflated in a manner which *Emma* never fully overcomes, in spite of the transformations of Charles's role later in the narrative from subject to opponent. The story of feminine desire remains linked consistently with the figure of the father, for the voice of the father always reverberates in the voice of the lover. The "position" Emma occupies here, as determined by the possessive adjective *votre*, and by her role as the object of a story in which the male formulates desire through the voice of the father, or functions as his symbolic equivalent, remains constant throughout the novel. Even as Emma becomes the teller of stories, she can exercise that role only in imitation of this initial model, within the structure of masculine desire.[9] The chapter ends with a paragraph in which the first sentence confirms the displacement of Emma as a subject of her desire: "*Emma eût, au contraire, désiré se marier à minuit, aux flambeaux*, mais le père Rouault ne comprit rien à cette idée." (24, italics added). The sentence derives as much meaning from its syntax as from its semantic content; the adversitive *au contraire*, which interrupts the verbal structure interrupts the language of Emma's desire, which in asserting itself against the father (lover) becomes disintegrated, deferred.

Shortly after her marriage, at the end of chapter 5, Emma's disappointments take the form of speculation about the full meaning of the words of love; they remain in a pre-narrative mode:

Avant qu'elle se mariât, elle avait cru avoir de l'amour; mais le bonheur qui aurait dû résulter de cet amour n'étant pas venu, il fallait qu'elle se fut trompée, songeait-elle. Et Emma cherchait à savoir ce que l'on entendait au juste dans la vie par les mots de *félicité*, de *passion* et *d'ivresse*, qui lui avaient paru si beaux dans les livres.   (32)

From the outset, Emma's experience of desire is linked to the elusive meanings of words; access to pleasure and knowledge will "take place" in language. Language is doubly deficient, however; on the one hand it is always the discourse of the other ("ce que *l'on* entendait par les mots ...") never the unique property of the desiring subject. On the other hand, the words mark a radical flaw in the system. Scandalously, they require but utterly lack reference. This dilemma, as critics have shown, is a key element of *bovarysm*, a desire/writing which maniacally seeks the *mot juste* without the ultimate guarantee of a reality which would validate the relations of signification. In a general sense, the object of desire in Flaubert's novels retreats under the proliferation of the signs which are necessary to its representation.[10] These words also have a particular relation to narrative: they mark a pre-narrative moment for Emma, in which the signifiers of desire are presented as pure nomination, not yet engaged in a verbal sequence. This moment is in many ways similar to the intransitive position which Anna O., in Breuer's famous analysis, assumes in her reveries, at one stage in her treatment. During her "absences," Anna murmurs the impersonal "tormenting, tormenting." Anna has lost the position of grammatical subject; she repeats an impersonal form with no immediate link to the first person, standing outside any narrative ordering of a fantasm.[11] Emma, too, at this point in the story has not yet appropriated a discursive form which will be charged with giving meaning to the signifiers of desire. The experience of desire here is the interpretation of the already spoken or written, which the subject cannot know until she assumes a relation to narrative.[12]

The retrospective account of Emma's emotional formation, in chapter 6 of the first part of the novel, is the story of her first seduction, the seduction by romantic fiction. The terms which refer to Emma's readings have significant erotic implications not simply in their themes, but in reference to the act of reading itself. The narratives of desire are invested with erotic intensity not only because of their content, but also because they are read in secret. Of reading keepsakes it is said: "Il les fallait cacher, c'était une affaire ..." (35). Erotic transgression thus becomes linked from the

48

outset with concealment and an intimate relation is established between narratives of desire and secrecy.

Emma not only fantasizes by imitating the stereotypes of romantic fiction throughout the novel, but her imaginings imitate the second-rate copy. Her representation of romantic fiction will be associated not only with erotic intensity, but also with the dissolution of energy. The texts which establish the models of desire are themselves set in a structure of destructive repetition. Emma reads the classics of romantic fiction, yet she reads with even greater pleasure the second-rate reproductions of romantic stereotypes; keepsakes and popular novels. By interiorizing the stereotype it becomes a fantasm, which Emma assumes as her personal history. The text does not repress the knowledge of the repetition, which implicates an omniscient narrator as well as the protagonist; it becomes one of the major motifs of the novel. In demystifying Emma's blindness to her engagement in these repetitions, the narrator assumes a largely sadistic role, which we may suspect is the effect of a powerful nostalgia for the lost power of now obsolete stories of desire, still painfully contemporary.

The relation of desire to language here is similar to that discussed above in the context of Emma's wish to know the meanings of the words of bliss, but there are significant differences. Attention shifts from the static paradigm (metaphor) to the mobile syntagmatic order of narrative (metonymy). Desire, when associated with the nouns which serve as its signifier, can only remain virtual, a possibility forever suspended. When it is articulated as the narrative of fulfilled pleasure, however, desire is linked inevitably with the alienating repetitions of the stereotype. The private strategy of concealment only renders more apparent this alienation within romantic narratives.

Other constants of Emma's relation to desire and narrative are also established in this chapter. Desire is experienced as an imperative to appropriate objects for personal profit. Emma's personal narratives will later provide the means for that appropriation, but here the motif of the pleasures of reading and the motif of appropriation are simply contiguous, not yet joined explicitly as they will be later in the novel. Certain links between the personally pleasurable and bourgeois economy, however, are already formed in this chapter:

Il fallait qu'elle pût retirer des choses une sorte de *profit personnel*; et elle rejetait comme *inutile* tout ce qui ne contribuait pas à *la consommation*

49

immédiate de son coeur, étant de tempérament plus sentimental qu'-
artiste. . . (34, italics added)

Pleasure is set in a system of exchange which conflates the
emotional and the commercial, in which the subject seeks to
consume the object of desire. Flaubert's correspondence
repeatedly underscores implications in this passage that Emma is a
perverted emblem of the artist and that her experiences of desire
are characteristic of bourgeois sensibility. Desiring, for Emma, is a
form of imitation whose object is the recuperation of sense, without
difference or loss.

In terms of the novel's narrative order, this chapter is analeptic to
the main narrative, its events situated in the protagonist's childhood.[13] Clearly, chapter 6 provides information about attributes of
Emma's "character" which will remain remarkably static
throughout the novel. Emma will attain maturity as a "subject,"
however, only when she actively orders the elements of Romantic
narratives according to an economic and sentimental schema
already set by these earliest reported experiences of literature.

In the remaining chapters of Part One, Emma's desires are
confined to a narcissistic silence. She now spins out her narratives
as voiceless fantasies. In the opening lines of chapter 7, Emma
composes hypothetical stories of travel to far-away places:

il eût fallu, sans doute, s'en aller vers ces pays à noms sonores où les
lendemains de mariage ont de plus suaves paresses! Dans des chaises
de poste, sous des stores de soie bleue, on monte au pas des routes
escarpées, écoutant la chanson du postillon, qui se répète dans la montagne avec les clochettes des chèvres et le bruit sourd de la cascade. (38)

Moments of daydreaming such as this, as Genette notes in an
excellent study of description and narrative in Flaubert, are doubly
silent.[14] The protagonists have ceased to speak to each other;
Emma turns toward the world of her dreams. The narrative of the
novel is also silent here, immobile, interrupted by a fantasy
narrative which suspends the sequence of events in the main story.
Emma's narratives, although they intrude upon the sequence of the
main story, never acquire the power to take over from that story the
initiative for ordering events.

Following this passage, the text focuses specifically on the
illocutionary context of communication: Emma's needs are formulated less in terms which characterize a specific object of desire than
in terms of a discursive situation.[15] She lacks that *other*, necessary
to the circuit of communication:

Peut-être aurait-elle souhaité faire à quelqu'un la confidence de toutes ces choses. Mais comment dire un insaissible malaise, qui change d'aspect comme les nuées, qui tourbillonne comme le vent? Les mots lui manquaient donc, l'occasion, la hardiesse. (38)

This passage opens up questions considerably more complex than the problem posed for Emma by the absence of an interlocutor. On the one hand the role of the other can never fulfill the function which Emma desires, for the other is to be always elsewhere and different from what the subject wishes. The images and the stories of desire, furthermore, are to be located beyond a particular and immediately accessible reality, a particular time and space contemporary to the subject, yet they can be constructed only with the aid of what they attempt to reject: reality . . . *another* reality. As for the formation of images and stories of pure desire, a further paradox makes itself felt. From the outset, there is a fundamental problem: these things, objects of desire, are lacking, and the elements which might constitute objects are heterogeneous, disparate, incapable of acquiring a stable configuration. Language cannot fix them, nor can they be generated by "reality" to be retrieved by language.[16]

Emma's attempts to arouse passion in herself pursue an illusive, provisional and ultimately inadequate solution. She develops theories about desire, narrative explanations of the empty signifiers. She repeats passionate verse in the manner of a sentimental catechism:

d'après des théories qu'elle croyait bonnes, elle voulut se donner de l'amour. Au clair de lune, dans le jardin, elle récitait tout ce qu'elle savait par coeur de rimes passionnées . . . (41)

Theory, for Emma, is auto-erotic, a solitary gesture directed toward narcissistic fulfillment. Knowing pleasure is repeating *by heart* the language of another's passion.

The major "event" of Part One, the trip to the chateau de Vaubeyssard, the dinner and the ball, appears to provide the occasion or access to the passion about which Emma had mused earlier. She remains excluded, however, from the language of potential partners in communication. What she wishes for most fervently is a passionate interlocutor, yet, in the conversations which take place in this sequence, she occupies an unmistakably marginal position; the language of the people at the chateau is incomprehensible, foreign to her. Emma is excluded because she is ignorant of the meanings of the speaker's words who "causait Italie":

A trois pas d'Emma, un cavalier en habit bleu causait Italie avec une jeune femme pâle, . . . Ils vantaient la grosseur des piliers de Saint-Pierre, Tivoli, le Vésuve, Castellamare et les Cassines, les roses de Gênes, le Colisée au clair de lune. Emma écoutait de son autre oreille une conversation pleine de mots qu'elle ne comprenait pas. (48)

Her alienation is also figured by the space in which she is caught, a space between two centers of desire. Although the swirling movements of her dance with the Vicomte transform the swirling, formless malaise (*qui tourbillone comme le vent* . . .) into intense pleasure, Emma is excluded from the verbal articulations of desire which she seeks to know. Two passages specifically underscore the link between silence and the enforced solitude of Emma's desire. In the first, Emma composes a brief narrative about a cigar case of green silk, which Charles finds by the road on their return to Tostes. Emma supposes that its owner is the Vicomte; her fantasy narrative transforms the case into a fetishized object:

A qui appartenait-il? . . . Au vicomte. C'était peut-être un cadeau de sa maîtresse. On avait brodé cela sur quelque métier de palissandre, meuble mignon que l'on cachait à tous les yeux, qui avait occupé bien des heures et où s'étaient penchées les boucles molles de la travailleuse pensive. Un souffle d'amour avait passé parmi les mailles du canevas; chaque coup d'aiguille avait fixé là une espérance ou un souvenir, et tous ces fils de soie entrelacés n'étaient que le continuité de la même passion silencieuse. (53)

A cigar case here, is not "just" a cigar case. Once again, Emma's silent narrative is both erotic and the reproduction of the fabric of another text; she composes her story upon the already woven surface of a fetishized object. Paradoxically, however, in seeking a sense which would attain the continuity of "authentic" passion, meanings become a play of surface effects, incapable of evoking the desired presence. The fiction of desire, quite literally, is a fabrication which affirms distance, not presence; "Elle était à Tostes. Lui, il était à Paris, maintenant; là-bas!" (53). The desired moment of absolute presence (*maintenant*) is deferred, and metaphorized as spatial disjunction (*là-bas*).

Emma's taste for stories is not easily satisfied, however, and the inadequacies of this narrative produce more fiction, generated by a word which, in its very emptiness, can accommodate all meaning:

Comment était ce Paris? Quel nom démesuré! Elle se le répétait à demi-voix, pour se faire plaisir; il sonnait à ses oreilles comme un bourdon de cathédrale; il flamboyait à ses yeux jusque sur l'étiquette de ses pots de pommade.

. . .

Paris, plus vaste qu'un océan.   (53–4)

This passage maintains a certain structural symmetry with the end of chapter 5, in which Emma had speculated on the meaning of the words *félicité, passion* and *ivresse*, yet there are meaningful differences between the two contexts which are due to the increasing importance of narrative to Emma's desire. The passages are similar in that each is an act of denomination, the terms in each case being devoid of semantic substance. The word Paris here must be referential, but is meaningful only as a figure. *Paris* is as empty a signifier as the words of passion, yet a fantasmatic geography has replaced the atopical terms of bliss, and Emma's imaginings move closer to narrative. The term *Paris* justifies the fantasmatic representation of desire, for it has historical, topographical reference, but it only functions effectively as a signifier which can accommodate the projections of desire when it becomes detached from that reference.

The act of naming is followed by another debauchery of reading, similar to that in the retrospective chapter 6. In the later episode, Emma subscribes to "feminine" reviews and studies descriptions of Parisian decors in E. Sue, Balzac and Georges Sand; "y cherchant des assouvissements imaginaires pour ses convoitises personnelles" (54). The same desire to consume the text and the same relation between desire and writing of both the first (Balzac, etc.) and the second order (*le journal de femmes*) are asserted as before. Emma takes the realist project literally; if the word is able to represent adequately the essence of things, then that essence is available to appropriation as language. Emma wants writing without difference, a desire figured here by her turning away from the symbolic mode of romantic narratives toward realist description and, beyond that, toward the iconic figure of a map of Paris. She buys a map and traces imaginary walks through the city:

Elle s'acheta un plan de Paris, et du bout de son doigt, sur la carte, elle faisait des courses dans la capitale. Elle remontait des boulevards, s'arrêtait à chaque angle entre les lignes des rues, devant des carrés blancs qui figurent des maisons.   (54)

Like Félicité, in "Un Coeur simple," who asks to be shown the house of her nephew on a map of Cuba, Emma's interpretation of the map seeks the real, where there is only the surface of an iconic figure. Her misreading in this passage allegorizes the separation between figures of desire and referents. Emma's finger on this fetishized surface of the map attempts an impossible coincidence between her imaginings and the abstract surface on which desire has been projected.

It is at this time that Emma begins to wear an open house coat, buys paper and a blotter and dreams of *Charles* becoming a famous writer:

Elle s'était acheté un buvard, une papeterie, un porte-plume et des enveloppes, quoiqu'elle n'eût personne à qui écrire.　　　(56)

Emma fills the space of lack not by writing herself, but by displacing the feminine subject in favor of a masculine proper name, which is to assume phallocentric mastery and circulate within a bourgeois economy:

Elle aurait voulu que *ce nom de Bovary, qui était le sien*, fût illustre, le voir étalé chez les libraires, répété dans les journaux, connu par toute la France
(58, italics added)

At the very moment when Emma might begin to write, her enclosure by the bourgeois family permits access to writing through the name of the husband, which can circulate only in accordance with the laws of commerce. Emma has effaced feminine difference in favor of the workings of the *non(m) propre*.[17]

Emma has come full circle; having gained access to narrative as the medium of desire she now refuses the role of the writing subject and in her fantasies seeks to give over that role to a man. The "solution" takes the form of denial and displacement; it produces a re-emergence of desire in the symptoms of a "nervous disorder": "Elle devenait difficile, capricieuse ..." "Elle pâlissait et avait des battements de coeur" (62, 63). This sequence, then, repeats regressively the order of Emma's initiation to narrative; from symptom, to fantasm, to the nominal terms (*félicité*, etc.) to narrative ... the silenced narratives of desire have been reconverted into the symptoms of hysteria. At the end of Part One of the novel, Emma can give voice to her desire only through the "silent" metaphor by which she is strangled: "Elle eut des étouffements aux premières chaleurs ..." (59).

Denials, repetitions and "bad" ironies

As we saw earlier, the first chapter of Part Two contains a curious observation by an omniscient narrator which announces that the events about to be told are ultimately inconsequential. Having suggested that this metanarrative comment must be read not only in terms of its authoritative detachment from the story, but also as already interpreted by the fiction of the first part of the novel, we can now consider some further implications of this passage. That statement would seem to refer to the "emptiness" of Flaubert's subject, to Emma's radical superficiality and to the bankruptcy of bourgeois, romantic desire, yet a reader attentive to the questions raised above will speculate on other possible resonances of this statement. These remarks establish the existence of a demystified tale, a story assumed to be by an omniscient which works in opposition to Emma's mystified stories. There is an implied contrast between two types of narrators, those who understand the aporia of fiction and those who are blind to its illusions. We are well aware of Emma's tenacious and desperately deluded belief in the power of her stories to change things and to appropriate the objects of her desire, and so her place in this opposition would seem to be securely established. Although they do not erase it entirely, ironic effects are considerably more complex than this opposition would suggest.

The account of the arrival at Yonville and the description of the setting, an introduction in the realistic manner, are written from the point of view of an omniscient *on*, which would seem to strongly reinforce mimetic illusion. Even as it is asserted most securely, however, that illusion is undercut. Situated at the end of a narrative/descriptive passage immediately preceding the arrival of the Bovarys at Yonville, the passage serves as a conclusion to a prefatory sequence. It thus has the effect of a denial which affirms and sets an omniscient narrator in a homologous relation to Emma.[18] It is not possible, however, to dissociate completely that narrator's stories from a belief in the finality of narrative which, ultimately, resembles Emma's faith. The telos of stories re-emerges even in deconstructive narratives, even in fictions which allegorize the aporia of meaning. We must consider, then, the doubling effects between an omniscient narrator and the central protagonist not only from the perspective of sadistic control. The schema is also strongly masochistic, for the relations between narrator and story inevitably reproduce the same dilemmas ironized in the account of Emma's fictions. The very assertion of a lucidly controlled relation to narrative cannot resist yielding ultimately to narrative's seductions.

Much has been written about Emma's relation to language in

Part Two of the novel, particularly about the importance of literary stereotypes in her exchanges with Léon, her second lover.[19] The couple's conversations repeat the already worn language of Romantic love, ironically exposing as a delusion the desire for a transparent language of fulfilled self-expression. Their exchanges require, yet cannot locate, an "original" language. Conversations are played out in a phatic register and the contact there established dramatizes a radical lack at another level.[20] The couple's conversations, the fragments of Romantic texts which they repeat, are linked to an economic mode of exchange:

Ainsi s'établit entre eux une sorte *d'association, un commerce continuel de livres et de romances*; (93, italics added)

Emma, even as a desiring subject, is appropriated by the discursive structures of a system against which passion asserts itself.

The stereotype, as Felman, Gaillard and others have shown, sets the would-be unique subject in a depersonalized language, a common currency, in the very moment at which he or she seeks fulfillment.[21] The language of singular experience is the stereotype of Romantic passion, which promises the possession of the desired object, as indicated by these exclamations following Emma's first amorous encounter with her first lover, Rodolphe:

Elle se répétait; "J'ai un amant! un amant!" se délectant à cette idée comme à celle d'une autre puberté qui lui serait survenue. Elle allait donc posséder enfin ces joies de l'amour, cette fièvre de bonheur dont elle avait désespéré. (151–2)

As Emma fantasizes about her emotions, a cascade of the empty terms of passion burst forth: "Elle entrait dans quelquechose de merveilleux où tout serait passion, extase, délire . . ." (152).

Emma's identification with Romantic heroines, their language and the imitation of a *type* of adulterous lover further erodes her difference:

Alors elle se rappela les héroïnes des livres qu'elle avait lus, et la légion lyrique de ces femmes adultères se mit à chanter dans sa mémoire avec des voix de soeurs qui la charmaient. Elle devenait elle-même comme une partie véritable de ces imaginations et réalisait la longue rêverie de sa jeunesse, en se considérant dans ce type d'amoureuse qu'elle avait tant envié. (152)

Through identification with these heroines and their voice, Emma is effectively deprived of her own status as first person subject; *je* becomes homologous with *elle(s)*; the self is multiplied as other(s).

As she finally "possesses" what she desires, Emma is herself possessed by those she imitates ("des voix de soeurs *qui la charmaient*").

In registers which are superficially distinct, though similar at a more abstract level, both Rodolphe and Lheureux, the merchant (*marchand de nouveautés*), know and exploit the links between desire, narrative and appropriation. Lheureux's astuteness ("c'était un homme habile") consists in anticipating the conjunction of appetites which Emma's frustrated love for Léon in fact produces: "Les appétits de la chair, les convoitises d'argent et les mélancholies de la passion se confondirent dans une même souffrance ..." (101). This conjunction between erotic desire and commerce becomes more and more intimate later in the book, and, as we shall see, it has far-reaching consequences.

In this section of the novel, the episode which works out most fully this equivalency between the social/commercial and the private/sentimental is, of course, the famous scene at the *Comices agricoles*. As Rodolphe presses Emma with his passionate language, the orators at the fair extol public and commercial achievements. The irony in this sequence stems not so much from the discord between Rodolphe's and the orators' voices which alternate in the passage, and from the contrast between private, sentimental values and public virtues, as from their underlying similarities; the register of sentimental exchange is not essentially different from that of the comices. In the collapse of an apparent opposition, public and private stereotypes which are superficially opposed are revealed as sustaining the circulation of similar values.

Rodolphe, for his part, knows something of the value of words and understands that seduction is a question of language.[22] His observations following one of his first encounters with Emma serve as a cruelly ironic echo of Emma's earlier wish to know the meaning of the three words of desire:

Ça baille après l'amour comme une carpe après l'eau sur une table de cuisine. Avec *trois mots de galanterie* cela vous adorerait j'en suis sûr! Ce serait tendre, charmant! ... Oui, mais comment s'en débarrasser ensuite?
(122, italics added)

Once again, and in a vulgarly dramatic manner, Emma is reduced to an impersonal status (*ça, cela*) alienated from even the minimally individual form of the subject pronoun. These brief musings, in fact, contain the entire narrative of the affair, whose end is proleptically announced at its beginning: "Comment s'en débarrasser ensuite?" Like the stories of romantic passion, it is a story already well known and one which pre-supposes the necessity of narrative closure even at its outset. The hint here that Rodolphe's schemes have much to do with narrative plotting as a repressive strategy of containment is confirmed at the end of the affair. Rodolphe's remarks, then, have a particularly rhetorical resonance; naming Emma for what she was, he provides a clear temporal demarcation and a neat narrative closure; "C'était une jolie maîtresse!" (187).

Whenever Emma enters into a "new" relation with stories or writings, her role as subject is already codified, determined by the discourse, and it is invariably an alienated role. The chapter which precedes mention of Emma's impulsive correspondence with Rodolphe ("Souvent même, au milieu de la journée, Emma lui écrivait tout à coup . . ." 174) contains a passage about the "bad ironies" of adultery, which she pursues so avidly, and suggests that letter-writing can be interpreted as one of those ironies:

Elle se repentait, comme d'un crime, de sa vertu passé, et ce qui en restait encore s'écroulait sous les coups furieux de son orgueil. Elle se délectait dans toutes les ironies mauvaises de l'adultère triomphant.   (173)

In fact, Emma's letters are never part of the novel and so we must look elsewhere for signs of their content and of their effect upon the couple. The principal result of these letters, as the opening passage of chapter 12 indicates literally, is to generate presence. This passage is almost a parody of Emma's insistent desire that writing produce a presence susceptible to appropriation; her letters summon Rodolphe to her side, but what really counts is the production of more narrative. Disgusted by her life with Charles, Emma writes Rodolphe impulsively, in the middle of the day, calls Justin to deliver the note, and Rodolphe appears . . . to listen to Emma's stories, her plans to escape:

Rodolphe arrivait; c'était pour lui dire qu'elle s'ennuyait, que son mari était odieux et l'existence affreuse! . . .

. . .

Elle soupira: "Nous irons vivre ailleurs . . . quelque part . . ."   (174)

On one level, letter writing is a "bad irony" of adultery, a liberty required by the transgression, exemplified elsewhere by other episodes such as the lovers' meetings in Charles's consulting room. The ironies are "bad" in other and more powerful senses, however, in that they subvert the control of the subject in the very exercise of her desires, according to patterns already elucidated. The permutations are many, but the operative figure here is ironic reversal, in which the difference between marriage and adultery is virtually effaced. The lovers' passion loses energy and becomes a "domestic flame" (159). In pursuing her desires, Emma loses all control as subject, and becomes subjugated to her lover:

avec cet supériorité de critique appartenant à celui qui, dans n'importe quel engagement, se tient en arrière, Rodolphe aperçut en cet amour d'autres jouissances à exploiter ... (170)

The fantasy narratives which anticipate Emma's new life with Rodolphe in a different country undergo a similar transformation; the signifier of absolute difference comes to symbolize an indifferent continuity. Emma's fantasies about her life with Rodolphe are contrasted with Charles's dream of future happiness, in a passage which follows immediately the account of Charles's dreams of domestic enjoyment for himself, Emma and Berthe, their daughter. Charles's projects center on the accrual of capital and the preservation of the family:

Il pensait à louer une petite ferme aux environs, ... Il en économiserait le revenue, il le placerait à la caisse d'épargne; ensuite, il achèterait des actions, ... il voulait que Berthe fût bien élevée ... Il se la figurait travaillant le soir ... Enfin, ils songeraient à son établissement; on lui trouverait quelque brave garçon dans un état solide; il la rendrait houroupo; cela durerait toujours. (102)

Emma's dreams, however, appear radically different, as the narrator suggests: "elle se réveillait en d'autres rêves." The contrast is elaborated through an opposition between the diegetic space of the narratives, familiar and local for Charles, picturesque and foreign for Emma:

Souvent, du haut d'une montagne, ils apercevaient tout à coup quelque cité splendide avec des dômes, des ponts, des navires, des forêts de citroniers et des cathédrales de marbre blanc ... Et puis ils arrivaient, un soir, dans un village de pêcheurs ... C'est là qu'ils s'arrêteraient pour vivre ... (183)

While Charles's dreams are static, Emma's are full of energy and movement: "Au galop de quatre chevaux, elle était emportée depuis huit jours vers un pays nouveau, d'où ils ne reviendraient plus." Charles dreams of producing and conserving capital and of containing sexual energy within the social and economic unit of the family. Emma, on the other hand, fantasizes endless leisure. The very absence of social context in Emma's dreams of Romantic bliss, however, points to an ideological repression, underscoring once again the alienating effects of her fantasm; the desiring subject, in her dream of plenitude, is invaded by the depersonalized representation of bliss. However different they may seem, Emma's fantasies of appropriating the objects of fulfilled desire are congruent to Charles's desire to control emotional and monetary capital. The end result, for each, is the death of desire, a final and meaningless continuity. For Charles, this is an eternity of domestic bliss (*cela durerait toujours*) and for Emma ... the eternity of an exotic life domesticated by familiarity:

> Cependant, sur l'immensité de cet avenir qu'elle se faisait apparaître, rien de particulier ne surgissait: les jours, tous magnifiques, se ressemblaient comme des flots; et cela se balançait à l'horizon infini, harmonieux, bleuâtre et couvert de soleil. (183)

Emma's letters, like her dreams, also suffer a radical loss of meaning, as in the scene in which Rodolphe rereads some of her communications, along with those of former mistresses, just before he writes her to break off their affair. The process of loss is complex; on the one hand, in the letters from Emma which Rodolphe rereads, sentimental expression has been contaminated and replaced by the practical. The letters are likened to business letters; and again the sentimental and the commercial are conflated. Filled with details of their projected trip, the letters are "courtes, techniques et pressantes *comme des billets d'affaires*" (188, italics added). Rodolphe never gets around to reading the others ("les longues, celles d'autrefois"), he is distracted by mementos of other past loves; bits of hair, old bouquets and the like, dusty fragments, fetishes no longer charged with erotic energy. These objects are only capable of evoking fragmentary memories of his former loves:

> A propos d'un mot, il se rappelait des visages, de certains gestes, un son de voix; quelquefois, pourtant, il ne se rappelait rien.
> En effet, ces femmes, accourant à la fois dans sa pensée, s'y gênaient les unes les autres et s'y rapetissaient, comme sous un même niveau d'amour qui les égalisait. (188)

The memory of Emma is already caught in a play of imitation and repetition when, before reading her letters, Rodolphe looks at her miniature portrait and is unable to assert the primacy of his recollections of the original, over the copy:

Il y avait auprès, se cognant à tous les angles, la miniature donnée par Emma; sa toilette lui parut prétentieuse et son regard *en coulisse* du plus pitoyable effet; puis, à force de considérer cette image et d'évoquer le souvenir du modèle, les traits d'Emma peu à peu se confondirent en sa mémoire, comme si la figure vivante et la figure peinte, se frottant l'une contre l'autre, se fussent réciproquement effacées.   (187–8)

The dramatic posturing in the picture suggests that the Emma represented is once again playing a role, miming a stereotype of a woman in a portrait. The model, in short, isn't very original. The integrity of a unique individual subject, the "original," is seen here only as a figural inscription, with no priority over the copy, both figures suffering a similar "effacement." Neither the writing subject nor her letters survives the passage into a representation which was to have assured enduring communication. Emma's texts become absorbed into the general anonymity of the signs which bear the traces of past loves. One signifier can be arbitrarily substituted for another in the impersonal and now random discourse of spent passion. The portrait and the letters have become figures in an anaphoric series of fragments.

Repetitions become more frequent at the end of the second part of the novel, the most extensive play of repetitions being set forth in the episode at the opera. This scene thematizes repetition in its *mise en abyme* structures, as Emma reconstructs her own personal past in the story of Lucie de Lammermoor, and in the content of the stories superimposed within the episode. The introduction at the end of the sequence, of a "new" narrative, as Emma's and Léon's re-acquaintance inaugurates a "new" affair, leads to a further chain of repetitions. The concentration of repetitions in this scene is preceded, moreover, by a number of others; the first and most obvious is Emma's desperate return to reading in order to distract herself from Rodolphe's rejection. After receiving his letter, Emma falls ill with a nervous disorder which repeats the episode of her hysteria at the end of the first part of the novel. Although the mysterious sickness is attributed by Homais to an allergic reaction to apricots, contained in a basket sent by Rodolphe in which his letter has been concealed, her symptoms are not allayed by the diet prescribed, but by a religious conversion. The "cure" is effected by providing for the displacement of Emma's repressed desire onto religion, as it was in her childhood at the convent. Once again Emma's fantasies are sustained by frequenting second-rate texts, imitations of the great romantic religious writings sent to her by a bookstore specializing in devotional literature: "C'étaient de petits manuels par demandes et par réponses, des pamphlets d'un ton rogue dans la manière de M. de Maistre, . . ." (200). As before in Emma's childhood, the devotional and the sentimental merge in a voluptuous language, now more intensely erotic:

Quand elle se mettait à genoux sur son prie-Dieu gothique, elle adressait au Seigneur les mêmes paroles de suavité qu'elle murmurait jadis à son amant, dans les épanchements de l'adultère.   (200)

Emma's sentimental excesses are once again judged by the family to be threatening and, as at the end of the first part of the novel, the remedy proposed is a trip. Although the excursion to the opera is not purely analogous to the move from Tostes to Yonville, structural homologies do exist: a change of scene sets the stage for a new affair. In one sense this trip is an ironic deformation of Emma's failed project of escape with Rodolphe to an exotic refuge. The irony is complex, however, for the trip to Rouen produces results considerably different from those intended. The "cure" does not put an end to Emma's nervous disorder, but aggravates the "malady" in ways unforeseen by any of the participants. The excursion is intended to establish closure by arresting the symptoms of malady/desire, yet it will provide the basis for a "new" sequence, which repeats the same desires, and plays out virtually the same fantasy narratives, the same deferrals of satisfaction, the same uncontrollable effects of writing.

The theatre and her doubles

The scene at the opera is crucial to an interpretation of narrative repetition in the novel: Emma's musings, interpretation and fantasy projections dramatize a dilemma repeated throughout Flaubert's writings; the absolute impossibility of ever being original, and the persistent desire for the unique. The writer, as it is said in the early novella, *Novembre*, wishes to attain the impossible originality of the mythical romantic genius, yet he remains a copyist, whose writing reiterates fragments of the already written:

Oui, il m'a semblé autrefois que j'avais du génie, je marchais le front rempli de pensées magnifiques, le style coulait sous ma plume comme le sang dans mes veines; . . . parfois des idées gigantesques me traversaient tout à coup l'esprit, comme, l'été, ces grands éclairs muets qui illuminent une ville entière, avec tous les détails de ses édifices et les carrefours de ses rues. J'en étais ébranlé, ébloui; mais quand je retrouvais chez d'autres les pensées et jusqu'aux formes même que j'avais conçues, je tombais, sans transition, dans un découragement sans fond; je m'étais cru leur égal et je n'étais que leur copiste!   ("L'Intégrale," 254)

The episode at the opera is one of the most cohesive of the sequences in the novel which are devoted to Emma's fiction-making. Though more complex in the structure of its narrative composition and in the stratification of various levels of interpretation, the passage recalls in certain ways Rodolphe's contemplation of Emma's portrait. The relations between an "original" and its imitation by figural transpositions once again efface the "original." Subjective identity, primary meaning or uniqueness of desire, make no sense whatsoever. To read the scene at the opera, however, as an unproblematically ironic dismissal of a naive dreamer, unable to maintain even the most rudimentary distinctions between "fiction" and "reality," as we surely do to some extent, is to dismiss both the complexity of Emma's interpretations and the more troublesome implication that Emma's confusions may in fact inhere to all fiction-making.

The chapter begins under the emblems of repetition, which provide necessary descriptive details (the name of the opera, and the principal singer) and which serve at the same time as a sign of the importance of repetition in the following episode:

A l'angle des rues voisines, de gigantesques affiches répétaient en caractères baroques: *Lucie de Lammermoor* . . . Lagardy . . . Opéra . . . etc.
(206)

As an enactment and interpretation of repetitions, the episode engages some of the central questions of the novel. The sequence repeats the major sentimental themes of Emma's life, but more important to our interests, it raises the issue of the interplay of repetition in desire, narrative and interpretation. Once again, as Emma attempts to order her desire as a story she is alienated by the discourse in which she seeks to locate herself. This passage suggests that the desire for narrative and for its interpretation is not easily assuaged even as mystifications and mis-readings are revealed in Emma's fictions.

Emma's interpretations of the opera, *Lucie de Lammermoor*, enact a rereading of the novel by Scott, which she knows from her youth. Her emotions in this scene are again set in an intertextual network; she asserts her subjectivity by rereading a literary text. The fiction on stage, however, is not the "primary" text for Emma, but is arrived at by the detour of a memory of the prose. These two fictions are also supplemented by Emma's memories of her own

63

life, which become a text superimposed on the other two fictions. This superimposition undercuts not only esthetic distinctions, those between narrative prose and stage performance, but in a more radical subversion, disrupts the boundary between fiction and "reality," source and text. Although the episode presents Emma's relations to fiction as fraught with naive illusions, exemplified most dramatically by her confusion between the actor Lagardy, who performs the fiction, and the off-stage character, Lagardy, who becomes the subject of her own fantasy, the text also presents Emma's readings and narratives in a highly complex textual network.

The recapitulative structure of the scene retraces and reiterates the stages of Emma's sentimental history and re-enacts a repetition which provides the narrative "starting point" for the third section of the novel. She enters the theatre like a child ("elle eut plaisir comme un enfant . . ."),[23] rereads the libretto of the opera through the memories of her own childhood, becomes caught up in the music, recalls the earlier emotions for Léon and the affair with Rodolphe, and finally, exits from the theatre before the third act . . . the third part of the opera, and the third section of Flaubert's novel. The scene is thus at once a retrospective narrative, the story of a hypothetical past and a proleptic vision.

Emma first reconsiders her past life, then quickly supplements the fiction performed on stage by her own modalized, hypothetical narrative of a past which might have been. In this ideal past, Emma once again yields to the sure control of a man and to an economy of sentiment, which the term *placer* suggests is linked to a bourgeois, commercial exchange:

Ah! si, dans la fraîcheur de sa beauté, avant les souillures du mariage et la désillusion de l'adultère, *elle avait pu placer sa vie sur quelque grand coeur solide*, alors la vertu, la tendresse, les voluptés et le devoir se confondant, jamais elle ne serait descendue d'une félicité si haute.

(210, italics added)

The *placement* or investment which Emma fantasizes in a nostalgic past is in fact arrived at as a complex series of *dis*placements; as she finds her own story represented by Lucie's role. This displacement generates a fantasized personal past which transforms the desiring subject into an object of masculine desire. Emma, the spectator, identifies with the actress, imposes on the dramatic role a fictional personal past, and then imagines this twice displaced figure of her desire as the desired object of the actor Legardy. Emma has

64

become a disabused interpreter, however, who knows the deceptiveness of words. *Virtue, tenderness, voluptuousness* and *duty*, converge in a single word, *félicité*, whose meaning she now recognizes to be generated by the deceptions of art:

Mais ce bonheur-là, sans doute, était un mensonge imaginé pour le désespoir de tout désir. Elle connaissait à présent la petitesse des passions que l'art exagérait ... Emma voulait ne plus voir dans cette reproduction de ses douleurs qu'une fantaisie plastique bonne à amuser les yeux, et même elle souriait intérieurement d'une pitié dédaigneuse   (210)

Paradoxically, as a disabused reader, Emma is doubly vulnerable to self-deception, for she once again becomes caught up in the seductions of fiction:

Toutes ses velléités de dénigrement s'évanouissaient *sous la poésie du rôle qui l'envahissait* ...   (210, italics added)

The role takes over, in spite of Emma's initial lucid resistance; it is a means of access to the "real." This desire to possess the real produces more than a simple confusion between the "real" and the performance; it composes the real through the only terms available to the desiring subject, the figures of fiction:

entrainée vers l'homme par l'illusion du personnage, elle tâcha de *se figurer* sa vie ...   (210, italics added)

The effort to appropriate the "real" (*entrainée vers l'homme*) is given over to the suspect operations of fiction, the figures of narrative fantasy:

Ils se seraient connus, ils se seraient aimés! Avec lui, par tous les royaumes de l'Europe elle aurait voyagé de capitale en capitale, partageant ses fatigues et son orgueil, ramassant les fleurs qu'on lui jetait, brodant elle-même ses costumes ...   (210)

The shift from a discourse on the person of the protagonist to the artifices of fiction making is marked by the term *se figurer*, and by a description of a primitive text-making, as Emma imagines herself embroidering the actor's costume. The text appears to have reproduced "reality," as the narrative tenses shift from the hypothetical past conditional, to the imperfect, recounting Lagardy looking at Emma, and finally to the present: "il l'aurait regardé. Mais une folie la saisit: il la regardait, c'est sûr! Elle eût envie de courir dans ses bras ..." (211). This moment of confusion between fiction and the textual "reality" is thematized as a moment of madness (*une folie la saisit*). Madness, for Emma, is the inability to maintain

65

distinctions which she knows are essential; the figural and the referential commingle, beyond control. If madness is the desired confusion between the operations of fiction (which maintain the vitality of desire) and "reality" (a moment of "sure" communication), then "sanity" can only be restored by reinstating the differences which desire would seek to obliterate. Paradoxically, then, the moment of communication which would be the fulfillment of desire, is its death; the possession of the "incarnation of love itself" is madness. The falling curtain, however, restores Emma to her senses, by reinstating the difference between stage and spectator, and in the wider sense, by re-establishing conventional barriers which are the conditions upon which desire can live.

If narrative organizes desire according to a deluded ideal of subjective control and intelligibility, and if these lies of fictions are known to Emma, she will nonetheless deny what she has come to understand; that denial, as we have seen, engages her once again in a narrative of desire. At this moment Léon appears, and Emma seems to move definitely outside of the complex and confused web of fictions, to turn away from rhetoric, toward an object of desire represented as real. This rejection of fiction is signaled in several ways. First, Emma abruptly denies her earlier fascination with the Opera. As Léon joins Emma and Charles in the theatre, he asks Madame Bovary if the spectacle interests her and she replies: "Oh! non, pas beaucoup." She also finds the mad scene excessive, artificial:

la scène de la folie n'intéressait point Emma, et le jeu de la chanteuse lui parut exagéré. (212)

Emma's lack of interest in madness is deceptive. She had been seized by madness at the moment in which the boundaries of meaning are disrupted. This is the brief instant of transgression, which is quite different from the representation of madness on stage. The theme of madness is contained by the discourse of reason, which radically reduces its otherness. Emma's confusion between "reality" and fiction, however, conceals a profound insight into the negativity of "reality," which is only accessible to her through the operations of fiction. Her folly is not only that the stage becomes "real" for her and that the place of the spectator becomes a fiction, but that even within these reversed polarities each position is at once fictive and "real." Emma believes firmly in the divisions between fiction and reality, yet the locus of both the "real" (offstage) and of the fictive (onstage) accommodates indiscriminately the other term. Emma constantly seeks to maintain thresholds between fiction and "reality" and to go "beyond" fiction to "reality"; what she fails to understand is that the interest is not what lies "beyond" but in the instability of the threshold.

Emma rejects the representation of a madness which is not madness, but becomes caught up in a different kind of uncontrolled play at the very moment when she appears to reject fictions with the greatest lucidity. In deflecting her attention from the theatre to Léon it would appear that she re-enters the world of real passion. At this moment, however, when the distinctions between fiction and reality seem the clearest, the desiring subject becomes caught up in a most impersonal play of language and enters a network of substitutions. Léon takes the place of Lagardy and of Rodolphe and of all the vaguely characterized men she has fantasized. Indeed, beyond its obvious meaning, Léon's remark about Lagardy, suggesting that he will soon put on another show ("Il donnera bientôt une autre représentation"), can be read as preface to the third section of the novel which introduces another performance in which Léon, not Legardy, will act out an already well-established narrative, in a sequence no less rigorously structured than the opera. We are far from the madness of the earlier scene, but this repetition, in its un-rationality goes beyond an untroubling feminine "folly."

Repetitions and their ends

The third part of the novel opens with observations by an omniscient narrator about Léon's experiences with women, which prepare for the first extended, intimate conversation between Emma and her companion. Léon's decision to possess Emma places her in a series of conquests, homologous to the series of the figures of Emma's desire in which the clerk himself has already taken a place. Léon's resolve is made possible by his repeated successes, yet its price is the wearing away of emotional spontaneity: "*sa timidité s'était usée* au contact des compagnies folâtres ..." (215, italics added). The passage suggests once again that the pursuit of desire is an affair of language. Léon's initiative is not sparked by an explosion of erotic energy, the prelude to a passionate act, but begins in a more calculated manner as a speech act: "Il fallait, pensait-il, *se résoudre* enfin à la vouloir posséder" (215). The overtures to seduction begin not in the stirrings of the heart but by setting a certain register of discourse. Léon's disabused choice of a rhetoric of seduction appropriate to his partner ("on ne parle pas à l'entresol comme au quatrième étage" 215) further heightens the alienation produced here by the couple's relation to language. As in earlier conversations, the exchange is structured as an imitation of imitations. Now included in this web of repetitions is an inevitable imitation of Emma's earlier affair; in giving herself to Léon, as Sartre has noted, Emma parodies herself.[24] Léon mirrors Emma's melancholy which itself is set in a web of repetitions:

> Pour se faire valoir, ou par une imitation naive de cette mélancholie qui provoquait la sienne, le jeune homme déclara s'être ennuyé prodigieusement tout le temps de ses études. (216)

In contrast to their first conversations in Part One of the novel, both speakers now consciously exploit literary stereotypes; they order and edit their narratives for rhetorical effect:

> Car ils précisaient de plus en plus les motifs de leur douleur, chacun, à mesure qu'il parlait, s'exaltant un peu dans cette confidence progressive. Mais ils s'arrêtaient quelquefois devant l'exposition complète de leur idée, et cherchaient alors à imaginer une phrase qui pût la traduire cependant. Elle ne confessa point sa passion pour un autre; il ne dit pas qu'il l'avait oubliée. (216–17)

The literary character of the conversation becomes increasingly evident, as Léon recalls having found an Italian engraving of a Muse in a print shop:

> Il y a sur le boulevard, chez un marchand d'estampes, une gravure italienne qui représente une Muse. Elle est drapée d'une tunique et elle regarde la lune, avec des myosotis sur sa chevelure dénouée. (217)

The representation seemed to him a likeness of Emma: "Elle vous ressemblait un peu" (217). This Muse is emblematic of the stereotypically fictional mode of the lover's exchange and allegorizes the inevitability of imitation. The passage is unmistakably caustic in its demystification of Romantic love and of the alienating effects of language. Even as the narrator ironizes the devaluation of passion through its language, however, he comments, in an intensely nostalgic remark, on the destructive inadequacy of language, "car c'est ainsi qu'ils auraient voulu avoir été, l'un et l'autre se faisant un idéal sur lequel ils ajustaient à présent leur vie passée. D'ailleurs, la parole est un laminoir qui allonge toujours les sentiments" (218). This nostalgia for an ideal language and a true narrative which would coincide entirely with personal history has many echoes elsewhere in the text and produces significant implications about an omniscient narrator's own relation to narrative. As we shall see, the register of irony is extended considerably by such statements.

The depersonalization of Emma and her lover in Part Three is executed even more relentlessly than earlier in the novel, as are the links between alienation and male narcissism. Critics have noted that as Léon recognizes Emma when she arrives at their rendezvous in the cathedral in Rouen he identifies her not by name, but by the impersonal pronoun: "C'était elle!" (224). A few pages later, the famous carriage scene produces an even more forceful displacement. The episode is the account of the first sexual encounter between Emma and Léon, the most intense of subjective experiences, according to their rhetoric of romantic love. Emma and Léon roll through the streets of the city in a journey whose only purpose could be determined by the untold action which occurs within the vehicle, yet that essential interior is never described. On entering and leaving the carriage, Emma is presented in the most impersonal terms. Hesitating to get into the carriage, she is persuaded, "determined," by a word:

– Eh quoi! réplique le clerc. Cela se fait à Paris!
  Et cette parole, comme un irrésistible argument, la détermina.   (227)

At the end of the sequence it is not Emma who emerges from the carriage, but simply "a woman":

Puis vers six heures, la voiture s'arrêta dans une ruelle du quartier Beauvoisine, et une femme en descendit . . .

The loss of an identity presumed necessary to sentimental exchange is underscored also by a crucial lacuna in the sequence. The scene "within" is never described; the protagonists disappear into a *lourde machine* (227), which is at once the erotic couple and the carriage.[25] The reader's interpretation of the goings on within the carriage is entirely dependent on the surface effects of meaning. The text omits what the situation would seem to require most. Far from a euphemistic suppression, this absence points again with sadistic insistence to the destructive effects of certain "machines": the carriage (*la lourde machine*) takes its place with the rolling press (*le laminoir*).

At the height of their passion in Rouen, during Emma's first visits, the couple's intense pleasure is described as a commingling of selves in a pleasurable *possession*, which, as earlier in the sequence with Rodolphe, leads to the domestication of passion.

Ils étaient si complètement perdus en la possession d'eux-mêmes, qu'ils se croyaient en leur maison particulière, et devant y vivre jusqu'à la mort, comme deux éternels jeunes époux. (246)

The alienating effects of a will to appropriation of the other becomes more and more apparent in this passage; there is an eventual equivalence between the lovers and the objects of a bourgeois décor. An insistent series of adjectives in the following passage blurs the distinction between possession of the other and possession of the objects which surround the lovers:

Ils disaient notre chambre, notre tapis, nos fauteuils, même elle disait mes pantoufles, un cadeau de Léon, une fantaisie qu'elle avait eue. (246)

The passage sets up a metonymic equivalence between Emma and the objects on which Léon lavishes his attention.[26] His admiration for Emma's soul is equated in a comic repetition of a symbolist correspondence, with an object, her lace. "Il admirait l'exaltation de son âme et les dentelles de sa jupe." This displacement is pursued further, as "Emma" becomes for Léon a series of roles, which, like his mistress's lace, figure Léon's desire:

D'ailleurs, n'était-ce pas *une femme du monde*, et une femme mariée! une vraie maîtresse, enfin?

Par la diversité de son humeur, tour à tour mystique ou joyeuse, babillarde, taciturne, emportée, nonchalante, elle allait rappelant en lui mille désirs, évoquant des instincts ou des réminiscences. Elle était l'amoureuse de tous les romans, l'héroïne de tous les drames, le vague elle de tous les volumes de vers. Il retrouvait sur ses épaules la couleur ambrée de *l'Odalisque au bain*; elle avait le corsage long des châtelaines féodales; elle ressemblait aussi à la *Femme pâle de Barcelone*, mais elle était par-dessus tout Ange! (246)

The apparently meaningful diversity of these characterizations paradoxically underscores the radical reduction of the protagonist to a series of equivalent figures. Finding and naming the object of desire, beyond the apparent diversity of Emma's temperament "la diversité de son humeur" leads to the inscription of the letter of Léon's desire: "c'était le vague *elle*/c'était le vague L." The pronoun not only breaks away from the construct which is Emma's personality, as she comes to signify all idealized woman, but, at the same time, though a homonymic play suggests the letter which signifies the desiring male: Léon: L.

The play of the letter becomes caught up in the "bad ironies" noted earlier in the sequence with Rodolphe. Within transgression, the defied norms reassert themselves. In this sequence Léon becomes Emma's mistress: "Il ne discutait pas ses idées; il acceptait tous ses goûts; il devenait sa maîtresse plutôt qu'elle n'était la sienne" (258). Léon, as mistress, is also caught up in a reversal of the sense of the pronoun and letter: elle : L : : L : elle. This is not the circulation of differences in a bi-sexual love which disrupts oppressive sexual polarities; on the contrary, relations of dominance and appropriation within a certain schema of desire establish sexual non-difference on a masculine model. These transformations reaffirm enclosure, instead of producing destabilizing effects which would open up new possibilities for the erotic intensities of difference.[27]

The passage we have been reading deals in the most direct way with narrative and desire; Emma asks Léon at each rendezvous to recount the story of events which have occurred since their last meeting and she asks him to write love poetry in her honor ("des vers pour *elle*," italics added):

Il fallait que Léon, chaque fois, lui racontât toute sa conduite, depuis le dernier rendez-vous. Elle demanda des vers, des vers pour elle, *une pièce d'amour* en son honneur; jamais il ne put parvenir à trouver la rime du second vers, et il finit par copier un sonnet dans un keepsake. (258)

This entire passage is a complex of repetitions, of imitations of imitations, whose effects include not only a depersonalization of the desiring couple, as the poetry of love is (re)written as a copy, but the disruption of difference, as the desiring male takes on the role of a passive mistress. Far from breaking with the ideology which underlies the relations between appropriation and desire in the novel, the reversals in this passage reinstate the same relations without effecting any violence to the schema itself.

An episode immediately preceding the account of Emma's financial ruin underscores once again the exhaustion of meaning within the stereotypical discourse of Romantic passion. As in the sequence with Rodolphe, the illusion of difference is exposed, and the language of desire suffers a radical loss of sense, figured in this passage by the conjunction of music and *vacarme* and by the literal resonances of the term *platitude*, a leveling effect:

son coeur, comme les gens qui ne peuvent endurer qu'une certaine dose de musique, *s'assoupissait d'indifférence au vacarme* d'un amour dont il ne distinguait plus les délicatesses.
Il se connaissaient trop pour avoir ces ébahissements de la possession qui en centuplent la joie. Elle était aussi dégoûtée de lui qu'il était

71

fatiguée d'elle. *Emma retrouvait dans l'adultère toutes les platitudes du mariage.*

(269, italics added)

Characteristically, Emma seeks a literary solution in response to this dilemma. She has now acquired Rodolphe's knowledge regarding the difficulties of endings: "Mais comment pouvoir s'en débarrasser?" Rather than bringing the story to an end as Rodolphe had done earlier, she continues to write love letters to Léon, believing that writing is *appropriate* to her role. The role survives beyond passion and writing produces desire in the absence of the lover. It is no longer a question in this passage of exchanging letters, however, as it had been in the correspondence with Rodolphe. There is no mention of Léon's participation. These letters are Emma's final effort of appropriation and, as throughout the novel, the inability of writing to seize upon the meaningful object of desire simply produces more desire and more writing. Emma's letters now dispense with the figure of her correspondent altogether; her texts produce "another man," spectre of her desire. By repeating literary models in an interplay of image and displacement, the wished-for transparency of a fixed meaning has been replaced by an uncontrollable supplementarity:

Mais, en écrivant, elle percevait un autre homme, un fantôme fait de ses plus ardents souvenirs, de ses lectures les plus belles, de ses convoitises les plus fortes; et il devenait à la fin si véritable, et accessible, qu'elle en palpitait émerveillée, sans pouvoir néanmoins le nettement imaginer, tant il se perdait comme un dieu, sous l'abondance de ses attributs. (270)

Emma experiences the most intense sensations of pleasure as she evokes this ideal lover: "Elle le sentait près d'elle, il allait venir et l'enlèverait tout entière dans un baiser. Ensuite elle retombait à plat, brisée: car ces élans d'amour vague la fatiguaient plus que de grandes débauches" (270). The other, object of desire, is most powerfully "real" as a purely anonymous verbal construct.[28] Emma is caught by the force of her own words; the potentially limitless profusion of attributes is capable of generating an endless sequence of metonymic figures for her desire. While Emma believes in the power of words to represent an attainable object, she loses touch here; the object becomes "real" only when it is entirely displaced from "reality." Reality is subjugated to the law of desire by a radical break with that reference which was to have been the ultimate validation of Emma's language. It is precisely at this point that the ideological underpinnings of Emma's mystified relation to

72

language become most explicit; the question of writing and of Emma's place in a narrative, shifts from stories of romantic desire to the complex financial schemes of Lheureux in which she has become entangled. One kind of writing is substituted for another; in "exchange" for her letters to her lover Emma receives subpoenas and notarized documents, the following paragraph tells us. The "commerce" she originally established with Léon is displaced by a more literally commercial affair. Once again Emma is situated in a story already composed and she must now narrate her desires in opposition to an inescapable narrative enclosure.

At the end of the novel, Emma recounts to several men the story (*son récit*) of her financial ruin; she speaks to Lheureux (272), all the bankers of Rouen whom she knows (275), Léon (275), Maître Guillaumin (280), Binet (284), and finally to Rodolphe (287). As indicated explicitly in the episode in which Emma visits Rodolphe, she approaches each of these encounters with an awareness of the problems facing the story teller, the problem of beginnings and the wider question of narrative order and content: "Que vais-je dire? Par où commencerai-je?" (286). These narratives are surprisingly congruent to Emma's stories of Romantic desire, although the relation between the teller and knowledge has been inverted. Emma's stories attempt to transmit knowledge, rather than to acquire it, but they are nonetheless similar to the sentimental narratives in their attempt to reappropriate what has already been lost. Just as Emma's stories of passion are repetitions of literary stereotypes in which the desiring subject has already been displaced, this story of financial ruin has already been composed, as the episode with Maître Guillaumin indicates specifically. Emma cannot escape the literal resonances of the term *situation*. The tale of her circumstances places her, encloses her, or one might say sites her (cites) her:

> Monsieur, dit-elle, je vous prierais . . .
> – De quoi, madame? J'écoute.
> Elle se mit à lui exposer *sa situation*.
> Maître Guillaumin la connaissait, étant lié secrètement avec le marchand d'étoffes, chez lequel il trouvait toujours des capitaux pour les prêts hypothécaires qu'on lui demandait à contracter.
> Donc, il savait et mieux qu'elle *la longue histoire de ces billets* . . .
>
> (280, italics added)

The effects of Emma's writing in this sequence are clearly more tangible than her romantic fantasms; by signing promissory notes she has provided a capital for Lheureux. Once again, Emma, as the teller, is the already told. Her value as a "subject" is measured more precisely here in terms of the arbitrary monetary system, which can function only in the absence of individual specificity. There are significant differences however, between the stories of erotic desire and the narrative of capital. While the secret operations of sentimental discourses are always discontinuous with the "real," the exchange in which the story of Emma's ruin is played out is an underlying reality. The similarities between the two types of narratives, Romantic/erotic and capitalist, suggest a fundamental congruence between their aims and their operations. The terms of Romantic desire are apparently gratuitous, yet they are not dissimilar from the system of exchange in which Lheureux's cupidity is played out. Paradoxically the story of Emma's ruin has realized the goals of all of Emma's narratives: appropriation and closure. That stable sense ˙ ͻthal, however, for, when achieved, it allows no possibility of repetition and metonymic displacement, which are the vital forces of desire and narrative. Emma turns desperately to narrative invention as a way out, near the end, but to no avail: 'Il faudrait inventer une histoire qui expliquât les choses à Bovary. Laquelle?'' (285). Emma's suicide follows immediately her submission to the position she has been forced to assume in the "intrigue" composed by Lheureux and Guillaumin; another system of desire flourishes on the bankruptcy of Emma's desires for romance. The triumph of Lheureux's plot dramatizes ironically the death of the subject, at issue implicitly, as we have seen, in all of Emma's fantasms and narratives. Emma's suicide, in a sense, is tautological, after the fact; it ironically validates as a stereotypical act what has already taken place in the dual registers of the sentimental and the economic.

Commentators have often remarked that the description of Emma's death recalls in grotesque detail the ultimately destructive consequences of her fascination with writing. The first effects of poison come to Emma as the taste of ink: "Cet affreux goût d'encre continuait" (293). The realistic details of the episode in which Emma's body is being dressed for burial have metaphoric resonances which repeat the same association between death and writing; black liquids pour forth from her mouth: "Il fallut soulever un peu la tête, et alors un flot de liquides noirs sortit, comme un vomissement, de sa bouche" (307).

The novel does not end with Emma's death, however; I can best interpret here the issues I have addressed by returning to Emma's last words, which counter in their ambiguity the apparently killing effects I have just been considering. Her last utterance is a suicide note, the only letter whose contents are ever presented directly in the novel. The fragment included in the text, "Qu'on n'accuse personne ..." has extensive repercussions, as suggested earlier. The most striking effect of this imperative against interpretation, of course, is to serve as a powerful incentive to interpret. If the narratives of Emma's desire are to be read allegorically as commentaries on fiction, making this statement invites us to return to our interpretations once again and to reconsider the problem of the connections between Emma's deluded narratives and the status of the novel itself as writing. Just as the principal sequences converge on the death of the major protagonist, questions of responsibility and irresponsibility are introduced in a way which invites speculation on problems of interpretive finality and the effects of deconstructive narratives in this text. The registers of ethics and rhetoric are inextricably intertwined here. Emma's simple melodramatic statement generates a complex series of questions. First, the identity of the pronoun *on* can be read as addressing the surviving protagonists, the reader, and perhaps obliquely, an omniscient narrator as well; every interpreter is a potential accuser, and Emma's last clichéd utterance, may, in fact, loosen the paranoic constraints of a certain kind of criticism and put in question once again the often sadistic authority of an omniscient narrator. Whom might one accuse? Who is the accusor and what is the accusation? On an ethical level, this novel, which so relentlessly exploits the ironic topos of adultery is a criticism of both the repressions of bourgeois society and the impasses of Romantic passion, and is not to be read as an apology either for marital fidelity or for adultery. Equally clearly, it is unlikely that the remaining protagonists will attribute Emma's death to a murder plot. Rather than interpreting this statement exclusively in ethical or hermeneutic terms, it is perhaps more productive to read this fragment as a statement about readability and interpretive authority and to further extend our considerations of the ways in which interpretations and narratives are deconstructed by the texts.

Emma's narratives subvert their own telos, as we have seen. They take place in a story which, in so far as it is validated by the authority of an omniscient narrator, necessarily repeats the delusions it ironizes throughout the novel. Irony is produced not only by the controlled performance of a narrator demystifying Emma's relation to stories, but will also include reverberations of the same desires and impasses in the performance of the deconstructive narrative. The text thus contests narrative performance ... in the performance of narrative. The story of the delusions of stories is not outside the delusions it re-cites. If Emma's narratives attempt to create an ordered "subject" (both an "I" and a topic), and attempt to give substance to the words of desire, the omniscient narrator's story, as a narrative, is also caught up with the complex of desires which motivate stories. The relentless construction of a distance between an omniscient narrator and the protagonist not only validates the differences between them but also makes it necessary to account for their distressing similarities. Whatever sadistic elements there may be in the narrator's relation to the protagonist, there is also a reflexive masochistic component as well, for the novel both reveals the deluded relation with Emma's stories and the law and at the same time problematizes the relation of its own writing to the law.

Perhaps the most interesting and elusive irony of the novel is not that which marks the *distance* between the protagonist's dispersed subjectivity and the dispassionate effacement of an omniscient narrator, but an irony which, beyond the differences between narrator and heroine, reasserts similarity between them. Flaubert's realism is radically different from Emma's corrupted romanticism principally because it rejects without illusion or concession certain relations with desire, representation and appropriation which remain constant in Emma's fantasies, stories and loves. The story proceeds from the knowledge that the dispersal of things and the dissolution of the self is not to be remedied by language or by repeating as one's own the already constructed stories of romantic passion, yet the novel attests to a generalized, irremediable dispersal and dissolution of forms and the self from which an omniscient narrator is no more exempt than is Emma. The novel is a construct; its relentless pursuit of form is the chosen defense against the impasses of desire and the failures of romantic topoi. A lucid detachment from Emma's struggles, however, cannot resolve the displacements and dissolution, any more than can Emma's narratives of escape to the perfect shore. The fragmentation and consequent depersonalization of narrators is a strategy which is made in response to the problems I have been discussing, yet it is a "solution" which consistently raises questions about the authority of narrators. While demystifying Emma's narratives as fetishistic, like the fetishist, an omniscient narrator repeats the denial of castration which he "knows" to be deluded. Readers have shown that Emma stands in a particular relation to castration; her failed apprenticeship to writing is an attempt to become a "man," to reserve castration, to attain an effective power over meaning and refuse her relation to lack.[29] I would like to pursue further the question of Emma's relation to castration and to conclude with some speculative remarks about authority, narrative and desire.[30]

Freud's essay on fetishism has much to say about incompatible views on important subjects, subjects which are not dissimilar to those I have been discussing either in their contradictory force or in their importance.[31] The fetishist, Freud tells us, denies the fact of castration, the child's reluctant acknowledgment that the mother does not possess the phallus, and with the fetish object seeks a substitute for an inadmissable lack. The refusal is not an absolute refusal of the "reality" of castration; in fact, that "reality" is acknowledged. At the same time that the child admits the lack, however, it is denied by the erotic investment in the fetish. The power of the fetish to endure, its resistance, as Derrida shows, is produced by the way in which incompatibles are linked, so that they never attain the resolution of decidability.[32] In one sense, there is a powerful difference between an omniscient narrator's and Emma's relations to narrative and to castration; Emma persists in believing in the finality of narrative and submits to her belief, while that belief is consistently problematized by an omniscient narrator, by the plurality of narrative points of view and by other means discussed earlier. The novel constantly raises questions not only of Emma's relation to the law, but of the subjects of writing, desire, the law and the aporia of meaning. The deconstruction of the Romantic narratives of desire is not a "simple" ironic dismissal, however, for recopying the narratives not only reaffirms their persistent fascination, as the narrator in *Novembre* had already told us, but it also suggests the extent to which all narratives call in question the subject's relation to an impossible meaningful completion. Inevitably, the ironic treatment of narratives serves as an alibi for a fetish: reasserting the power of narrative and the impossible desire to make meaningful as one's own the empty words of bliss.

4

THE AUTOBIOGRAPHY OF RHETORIC: ON READING RIMBAUD'S *UNE SAISON EN ENFER*

" . . . ne sachant m'expliquer sans paroles paiennes, je voudrais me taire."
"Mauvais Sang," (214)

"J'ai eu raison dans tous mes dédains: puisque je m'évade! Je m'évade! Je m'explique." "L'Impossible," (235)

" . . . il me sera loisible de *posséder la vérité dans une âme et un corps.*"
"Adieu," (241)[1]

The three statements quoted above appear at significant junctures, and widely separated, in *Une Saison en enfer.* The first is in one of the opening sections of the text, "Mauvais Sang", in which the narrator attempts to situate a quest for self-knowledge in a specific relation to history. In the second passage, from "L'Impossible," the narrator begins to refuse certain social compromises. Finally, the words in the last quotation are the final words of the entire text, about a page and a half after the narrator's statements that he has finished recounting his season in Hell, and that he is now prepared to celebrate the birth of *la sagesse nouvelle.* Each one of the quotations, though in significantly different ways, situates the narrator's quest for understanding in the register of language. The confession in *Une Saison en enfer* is an interpretive process in which scrutiny of the poet's past and present, of history, metaphysics, love, writing, and so on, leads inevitably to an examination of the speaking subject as a configuration in language.

The text begins within the frame of certain assumptions about the finality of the written corpus and its capacity to contain the narrated subject; these assumptions are "worked out" as they are reiterated in the course of the narrative and ultimately exhausted. A radically different understanding of the writing subject emerges as the relationship between cognition and the language of the text becomes an increasingly urgent concern of the narrator. As the narrator produces the story of the past or the present, he explicitly performs a reading which deflects the interest from the (pseudo)-referential content of the text and toward the operations of language. That shift deconstructs a figure of the Romantic self, yet is concurrent with a forceful and nostalgic resistance to the process; much of the affective tension of the text is generated by these irreconcilable forces. Various aspects of the theme of alienation constitute an important network in *Une Saison en enfer* which can be interpreted within Romantic concepts of the self, yet a far more subversive alienation is at work in the language of the text, and it is the interplay between these forms of alienation, thematic and rhetorical, which I propose to trace here.[2]

In many respects, of course, the passages quoted above conform to the traditional patterns of an autobiographical narrative. The poem presents the narrative (*histoire*) of a season in hell, a passage through a subterranean world of past suffering, delusion and failed strategies for re-inventing love, literature and freedom, from which the poet emerges into the clear light of truth ("Matin"), or so it would seem, as the narrated self and the narrating subject merge in the present *discours*: "Pourtant, aujourd'hui, je crois avoir fini la relation de mon enfer" (239).[3] To the extent that we interpret the text according to this traditional schema of autobiographical writing, as defined by Genette, Lejeune, Rousset, Starobinski and others, the development of the narrative can be traced in the passage from the verb *je fis* of the narrated past to the verb *je sais* of the narration, situated at the end point of the story. The statements quoted earlier could be read as the expression of the concurrent desires to lead the reader through the text to the truth of the conclusion and to find the language adequate to that achievement; the passages would appear, then, to situate the text securely within the boundaries of this definition of confession narrative proposed by Paul de Man in a reading of Rousseau:

To confess is to overcome guilt and shame in the name of truth: it is an epistemological use of language in which ethical values of good and evil are superseded by values of truth and falsehood, one of the implications being that vices such as concupiscence, envy, greed, and the like, are vices primarily because they compel one to lie. By stating things as they are, the economy of ethical balance is restored and redemption can start in the clarified atmosphere of a truth that does not hesitate to reveal the crime in all its horror.[4]

Read according to this schema the quotations from Rimbaud would mark a progress toward truth in which the narrator had overcome the shortcomings of a deficient ("pagan") language, had countered the ruses of self-deception, and had found the happy reconciliation between desire and truth ("la liberté dans le salut," "Mauvais Sang") possessed in a final moment of the text. My reading thus far makes the text conform to a quite unremarkable rhetoric of autobiography, and anticipates, on the one hand, how consistently the narrator reproduces elements of that schema, which subtends the entire poem. On the other hand, the strategies of the text are quite different. They resist forcefully the implicit telos of such a rhetoric, in which the relations between *histoire* and *discours* are considered as a unity of becoming, oriented towards a final appropriation of truth in the consciousness of self. I propose to examine the narrator's developing relations to the text by studying some of the various ways in which the self is inscribed as an effect of writing in which each utterance of the first person pronoun produces a division of the self at the very instant it is posited.[5] As the narrator dismantles a certain rhetoric of autobiography in a practice referred to in the text as *délire* (which can be read both as delirium and dé-*lire*), the act of writing literally forces to the surface of the text the understanding that the narrating subject is engaged less in a process of self-realization, in the manner described by de Man, than in writing the self in and as language, and deprived of any reassuring ontological ground. In this sense, the practice of writing is not the expression of a self, contained by the rhetoric of autobiography, but the exploration of effects of subjectivity in language; the subject of writing, then, becomes the autobiography of rhetoric. My study will explore the implications of the imperative set forth in the final passage of the last text, "Adieu," – "Il faut être absolument moderne." In this context, and in the light of the problematic traced above, the statement "Je m'évade, je m'explique" takes on new resonances which suggest that self-realization in narrative necessarily gives way to an endless process of unfolding (the sense of *explicare*) and distancing.

Several references in the first two texts of *Une Saison en enfer*, the short preface which serves as a dedication to Satan, and the longer "Mauvais Sang," establish that the problem of language is central to the quest for self. The first act narrated in the poem is a speech act, a *performative*, in Austin's terms, which produces a violent break between the language of the text and the language of "Beauty."[6] The narrator recounts having taken Beauty upon his knee one evening and, finding her deficient, cursed her: "Un soir, j'ai assis la Beauté sur mes genoux. – Et je l'ai trouvée amère. – Et je l'ai injuriée," (211). Beauty here serves rather unexceptionally as a personification for art in general, and particularly for verbal art; thus, one of the very first narrated events of this text is a specifically verbal act, a violent repudiation in which the narrator attempts to dispossess himself of the muse. As a performative, this statement is itself the "event" to which it refers, and affirms truculently in the opening pages of the poem the overriding importance of the subject of language over non-linguistic reported action. Though the esthetic which Beauty personifies is not specifically characterized, as it will be later in the central section, "Alchimie du verbe," the initial refusal of her patronage is accompanied by a series of rejections which here and throughout *Une Saison en enfer* will be associated with cultural authority in general. The project of the text is twofold, set forth already in these first pages: to elaborate in detail the angry curses against Beauty, which will undo a cultural text, and to inscribe the narrator's self in a radically different relation to language.

The curse against Beauty is accompanied by a rejection of Law: "Je me suis armé contre la justice." The subject flees from the confines of defined space, in an escape which is also a flight from the self: "Je me suis enfui . . ." That displacement in space also places the subject outside hope: "Je parvins à faire s'évanouir dans mon esprit toute l'espérance humaine. Sur toute joie pour l'étrangler j'ai fait le bond sourd de la bête féroce." The refusal of Beauty, then, is followed immediately by a break between the narrator and a system of dominant cultural authority, the coordinates of a certain space and the confines of expectations which had defined the subject. From the outset, writing in this text is a rupture, a violent break with social order, which opens the question of the nature of the alternative space and order, the outside, in which the narrator will ultimately situate himself. That question, of course, provides the motive for the entire narrative, its "resolution" deferred to the end point of the text. For the moment, however, the text explores the impasses produced by the present order; the narrator will pass from esthetic considerations to the wider problematic of the relation between the self and order in its most general sense: the law. The explicitly esthetic consequences of these rejections are indicated in the last paragraph of the dedication, in which the narrator addresses Satan:

Mais, cher Satan, je vous en conjure, une prunelle moins irritée! et en attendant les quelques petites lâchetés en retard, vous qui aimez dans l'écrivain l'absence des facultés descriptives ou instructives, je vous détache ces quelques hideux feuillets de mon carnet de damné. (211–12)

Elliptically, but no less significantly, the passage reiterates the

81

rejection of Beauty and informs the reader about the new writing which that break makes possible; Satan's taste runs counter to mimetic or didactic writing. The relation of the narrator's text to truth, as a replication in language of a pre-existing sense, either a model reiterated in description or an ethical or epistemological meaning, is thus put in question from the outset. The consequences of this affirmation are far-reaching indeed; it opens the possibility of different kinds of meaning, produced in a counter-discourse which would disrupt the metaphysical closure which is the condition of mimesis.[7] The insistently absolute nature of the project must be interpreted from the beginning, however, with a certain irony, for in seeking Satan's patronage the narrator has simply reproduced the dilemma which was to be resolved by the rejection of Beauty. One patron has taken the place of another and it might be suspected that subscribing to Satan's authority is in many ways congruent to accepting the laws of Beauty. This gesture of revolt then becomes symptomatic of the same dilemmas against which the narrator proposes to write. We may suspect that the narrator is not altogether mystified, for there is a melodramatic note of self-mockery in this passage ("cher Satan, je vous en conjure, une prunelle moins irritée ... ") which raises the possibility that the "solution" proposed is not as resolute as it appears. The title of the text, *A Season in hell*, confirms the provisional character of this patronage, and suggests that this authority is indeed temporary and that one of the central issues of the poem will be the relation between language and the mastery over meaning. If the narrator is to emerge from the season in hell, we may assume, it will be by rejecting any transcendental authority over meaning, whether it be that of the conventionally negative Satan or of the positive figure, Beauty.[8]

The next section of *Une Saison en enfer*, "Mauvais Sang," explores the narrator's estrangement from the dominant truths of an ideological system from which he is irrevocably excluded. The poem recounts a failed quest for origins, in which the narrator seeks a place for the self within the enclosure of a history and its metaphysics, yet repeatedly finds that his "place" lacks the desired centrality. He is constantly dis-placed toward the uncertain space of the shifting margins of the system. This marginality is figured throughout the passage, not only by the themes of bad blood, idolatry, sacrilege, idleness, vice and other similar ethically or economically determined alienations, but also as a complex relation of the narrator to language. That relation is the interplay between the language of the "real world" and the strategies which the narrator comes to discover operating in his own language. In both these registers, thematic and rhetorical, the poet is repeatedly displaced from the position of centrality which he claims to seek. This dislocation can be considered in terms of the idiom which the narrator calls a perfidious or pagan language and, concurrently, in terms of the relations of the narrating subject to past cultural and personal history and its language. This inquiry leads to an investigation of the problematic relations between *histoire* and *discours* in this text and the attendant disruptions of the model of autobiographical narrative alluded to earlier.[9]

In the opening lines of the poem, the narrator rejects all links between writing and any useful social activity. This anti-utilitarian stance can scarcely be taken for the idealism of Art for art's sake, however: "J'ai horreur de tous les métiers. Maîtres et ouvriers, tous paysans, ignobles. La main à plume vaut ... la main à charrue. Quel siècle à mains! Je n'aurai jamais ma main" (213). The poet violently dismisses a mode of writing which would ground the self in an established social order, its discursive practices and its cultural norms. An alternative practice of writing would subvert that order, yet neither here nor elsewhere does the poet propose a program or poetics of that mode. As we shall see, any esthetics of disruptive writing is mystified from the outset, for attempts to systematize that activity reinstate the control which the counter-discourse seeks to undermine.

In "Mauvais Sang," the poet repudiates all manifestations of domesticity, including the *specular figures*, mendacity and criminality. "Après, la domesticité mène trop loin. L'honnêteté de la mendicité me navre. Les criminels dégoûtent comme des châtrés: moi, je suis intact, et ça m'est égal" (213). The term *intact* here figures an (impossible) escape from castration; the narrator supposes that he is outside the law of the Father. It is that unique position, both privileged and deficient, which he will seek to escape, while refusing submission to the particular order of western civilization. For the condition of being intact is the lure of *in*difference ("ça m'est égal"), as though the subject could exist outside the constraints of any discourse whatsoever, be identical to its own undivided psychic components ("*ça* m'est égal"), or outside of any articulation between the subject and its relation to a lack.[10] The possibility of this phallic plenitude is belied, however, by the narrator's persistent desire to situate the self in a relation with history, the lineage of his fathers, and language. "Si j'avais des

83

antécédents à un point quelconque de l'histoire de France. Mais non, rien." Failing to find that link, the narrator unsuccessfully seeks a place in the continuous narrative of the nation's institutions, the church, or in the more immediate past of personal history; he is repeatedly dislocated, thrown back into the present and into what he variously characterizes as a treacherous or pagan language. The issue is now no longer the absence or want of lack, but the relation to be assumed to that want which acknowledgment of lack makes necessary.

Pagan discourse, the narrator's alienated "language," is never explicitly defined, yet it is characterized negatively by a system of exclusions. Most importantly, pagan language is the language of the present, of *discours*, discontinuous with the narrated past of the nations: "Je ne me souviens pas plus loin que cette terre-ci ... " (214). Concurrent to this amnesia is an exclusion from the language of the past. The dominant authority of the present is continuous with the "real" history of the past, and there is no break between the language of the past and that of the present. The poet, on the other hand, is excluded not only from the past, its language and its narrative, and the language of the present, but he does not know the language of his own recent past: "toujours seul; sans famille; même quelle langue parlais-je." The pagan tongue is not only outside of the family, it lacks the ultimate transcendental basis: "Je ne me vois jamais dans les conseils du Christ ... " "Freedom" from the symbolic father is presented here in several variants, as detachment from the church, law, nation, reason and science, yet the poet is nonetheless left with a powerful nostalgia for origins.

"L'Esprit est proche, pourquoi Christ ne m'aide-t-il pas, en donnant à mon âme noblesse et liberté. Hélas! L'Evangile a passé! L'Evangile! L'Evangile!

J'attends Dieu avec gourmandise, Je suis de race inférieure de toute éternité" (215)

The quest for self is articulated as a quest for both an authentic past and a language capable of containing and reproducing its truth. The narrator formulates this search in the remaining passages of "Mauvais Sang" as a relation to history, in the conventional sense, as a master narrative, and also in the more precisely linguistic sense (*histoire*), as the language which relates past events. The meaningfulness of the narrating *I*, in discourse, is not to be found here in the language of the present, for this utterance is devoid of truth. In the manner of a classical autobiography, the narrator turns to *histoire*, in an effort to reconstruct a present identity which would be produced as the subject describes and evaluates the errors of the past. By maintaining a separation between two linguistic moments, the narrated past and the present of narration, the narrator would find support for the analysis in the present and determine a coherent relation between two instances of the subject. The effort to know in the present is thus dependent upon initially maintaining a separation between discursive levels; only by traversing that space between the two levels can the analysis arrive at the abolition of that distance, in the desired unity of self-knowledge. These efforts, however, merely repeat the impasses I have been discussing; every excursion into a narrated past becomes literally ruined by the invasion of verbal and adverbial forms linked to *discours*, the present of narration. The narrator must now either turn toward exploring how the self is alienated in the language of the present, or turn toward fantasmatic solutions which deny the dilemma already uncovered.[11]Whether in recounting the past or inventing a future, the text is unable to sustain long sequences of narrative which depart from *discours*, and the narrator is quickly cast back into the inadequate language of the present. The attempts to place the self in the past should be marked by a shift from the present tense of narration to the past definite of *histoire*, but the epistemological and ontological authenticity of the past events are eroded by the use of a hypothetical mode, the past conditional:

"Je me rappelle l'histoire de la France, fille ainée de L'Eglise. J'aurais fait, manant, le voyage en terre sainte . . . Plus tard reître, j'aurais bivaqué sous les nuits d'Allemagne".   (214)

Even the tenuous mimetic illusion of these narrated actions is soon undermined, as the narrator is forced to return to the time, space and language of the present: "Je ne me souviens pas plus loin que cette terre-ci . . . "

The failure of *history/historie* to provide a stable signified as meaning in the present is echoed in a thematic register in the treatment of the theme of progress. The linear development of civilization according to an historical telos, as a tradition of truth and development of knowledge, would be homologous to the anticipated development of the individual. That structure is also disrupted, its telos put in question: "La science, la nouvelle noblesse! Le progrès. Le monde marche! Pourquoi ne tournerait-il pas?" (214). The confrontation between the idea of progress and the understanding of the finiteness of man and nature, a major preoccupation of nineteenth-century thought, is here given over to the operations of rhetoric and to the hazards of the arbitrary logic of word play.[12] The narrator's rhetorical question ("Le monde marche. *Pourquoi ne tournerait-il pas?*") is more than an ironic quip which reactivates the cliché of the world striding toward progress. The sense of self is here to be found less in the full meaning of the grammatical sense of the passage than in the operations of rhetoric, which makes it impossible to decide whether the narrator is or is not posing a serious question. It is not possible to say whether the text proposes an opposition between a cyclical and a linear view of history, or whether the narrator just doesn't care. It has been argued that this confrontation between grammar and rhetoric opens up wide-ranging questions about the decidability of meaning in literature.[13] Here that shifting meaning further erodes the possibility of the narrator finding a stable ground for the expressive self in history, and situates the quest in the impersonal operations of language.

In the passage immediately following this one, the self is projected into a fantasized future by means of a predictive narrative, only to find that this prophetic future is symmetrical to the failed invention of a meaningful past. It is a similar deflection of the self away from a deficient present and to its diegetic space:

Me voici sur la plage armoricaine. Que les villes s'allument dans le soir. Ma journée est faite; je quitte l'Europe. L'air marin brulera mes poumons; les climats perdus me tanneront.

. . .

Je reviendrai, avec des membres de fer, la peau sombre, l'oeil furieux: sur mon masque, on me jugera d'une race forte. J'aurai de l'or: je serai oisif et brutal. Les femmes soignent ces féroces infirmes retour des pays chauds. Je serai mêlé aux affaires politiques. Sauvé.

Maintenant je suis maudit, j'ai horreur de la patrie. Le meilleur, c'est un sommeil bien ivre, sur la grève.

. . .

On ne part pas. Reprenons les chemins d'ici . . .   (215)

The movement from now and here, to another time and place fails with equal decisiveness, whether the narrative is retrospective or predictive.

A third narrative sequence recalls the narrator's recent past, the "real past" of his childhood, and it also lacks the power to provide the meaningful ground for self-presence. The wanderings in the recent past are as futile as the mythical projects just recounted:

Sur les routes, par des nuits d'hiver, sans gîte, sans habits, sans pain, une voix étreignait mon coeur gelé: "Faiblesse ou force: te voilà, c'est la force. Tu ne sais ni où tu vas ni pourquoi tu vas, entre partout, réponds à tout. On ne te tuera pas plus que si tu étais cadavre." Au matin j'avais le regard si perdu et la contenance si morte, que ceux que j'ai rencontrés *ne m'ont peut-être pas vu*. (216)

The image of the transparent self figures the absolute lack in substance of the narrated *I*, and plays with a topos of confession narratives in a manner which forcefully undercuts its traditional function. According to the stereotype, the narrator proposes to unveil his past self in order to reveal the truth in all its nakedness, as in the opening pages of Rousseau's *Confessions*. In Rimbaud's text, however, unveiling the self fails to provide access to a plenitude of meaning. Paradoxically, the pure transparency of meaning is literally meaningless; the self which has found no place in the language of the other is utterly devoid of significance.

Further on in the same sequence the narrator again rejects the laws of authority, yet the claim to absolute alterity does not produce a reassuring sense of self-sufficiency. The narrator is again cast up into a meaningless present.

Prêtres, professeurs, maîtres, vous vous trompez en me livrant à la justice. Je n'ai jamais été de ce peuple-ci . . . Je ne comprends pas les lois; je n'ai pas le sens moral, je suis une brute: vous vous trompez . . .
(216–17)

Following this failure to establish a patrilinear link with a past origin, the narrator once again projects a proleptic narrative as a mythical future. The irony of the episode in which the poet adopts the persona of a cannibal saved by white colonialists is hardly intricate: "Les blancs débarquent. Le canon! Il faut se soumettre au baptême, s'habiller, travailler. / J'ai reçu le coup de la grâce" (217). The uncomplex irony of the opening of this sequence, in which the savage is a figure for childlike innocence ("Vais-je être enlevé comme un enfant, pour jouer au paradis . . . ?"), becomes more problematic as the allegory is abandoned. Returning to narration in the present, the narrator's pronouncements are advanced as the sole validation of his innocence: "Apprécions sans vertige l'étendue de mon innocence . . . Je ne me crois pas embarqué pour une noce avec Jésus-Christ pour beau-père" (218). The narrator formulates his desire simply; what he wishes to attain is truth and salvation now, a pure logocentric self-presence, an absolute and unmediated origin in the present: "Je ne suis pas prisonnier de ma raison, J'ai dit: Dieu. Je veux la liberté dans le salut" (218). The self is fully present in the closure of its own discourse ... but it doesn't last. The narrator recognizes that his pronouncement, in its repetition of the inaugural moment of creation, has produced not the desired moment of pure truth, but farce: "Farce continuelle! Mon innocence me ferait pleurer. La vie est la farce à mener par tous" (219). Farce then, is the explosive recognition that attaining the coincidence of self and language is merely the deluded repetition of an origin which never existed. [14]

In the patterns I have been discussing, writing systematically explores the resources of certain rhetorical possibilities and plays out their deficiencies, returning the narrator to a *discours* incapable of either retrieving or producing what it seeks. Increasingly, the text will force the realization that the only language available to the narrator is one in which each articulation of *I* produces the mark of non-coincidence, which deconstructs the ideal of an expressive self and narrative telos which subtends the search for meaning and presence.

I can now briefly and elliptically outline a reading of the rest of *Une Saison en enfer* in terms of the problematic discussed above. The discovery becomes increasingly explicit that desire for "absolute modernity," and the concurrent rejection of past errors, repeatedly engages the narrator in an interpretive process in which the function of language, and most specifically, the language of *discours*, is the central issue. To be "absolutely modern" will result from rejecting a deluded relation to *histoire* and posing the question of modernity in the register of *discours*. The first effort will be to demystify the poet's earlier attempts at modernity, illusions about love and about literature; only then will the way be cleared for establishing a "new modernity" as a new relation to language. It will be seen that the narrator accomplishes this by "writing himself out" of *histoire*, so to speak, primarily in the two central texts of "Délires," which are presented explicitly as confession and *histoire*. Only then does he turn to the present of narration, as narrative becomes displaced by *discours*. Paradoxically, in those sections in which the narrative conforms most closely to the patterns of confession, maintaining a separation between a narrated "real" past and the present of narration, the sense of discontinuity between different moments of the subject's story becomes increasingly strong. The radical otherness of temporally distinct moments of the story, and the lack of ontological links between the narrated and the narrating *I*, serve to erode further and further the rhetorical conventions of autobiography.

In "Nuit de l'enfer," the few passages which narrate a complete past are all variants on the theme of past delusions now rejected. The shift to the level of *discours* is concurrent with an explicit judgment on the delusion of having attempted to find meaning in history, and we may assume, in attempting to find meaning *as* history.

"J'avais entrevu la conversion au bien et au bonheur, le salut. Puis-je de décrire la vision, l'air de l'enfer ne souffre pas les hymnes. C'était des millions de créatures charmantes, un suave concert spirituel, la force et la paix, les nobles ambitions, que sais-je?" (220)

"plus de foi en l'histoire" (221)

Repeatedly thrown into the space and time of the narration, the only moment and place in which meaning can be situated, the narrator interprets the conjunction of the present of discourse with the narrated self as a displacement from the world. To be outside of the world is to be outside of meaningful time: "Ah, ça! l'horloge de la vie s'est arrêtée tout à l'heure. Je ne suis plus au monde" (221). Rather than living in a continuity of becoming, the narrator knows the present as the immediacy of discontinuous moments, set adrift from temporal sequence. The subject is irrevocably fragmented, at once affirming and denying its own existence and situation: "Il n'y a personne ici et il y a quelqu'un ... " (221). "Je suis caché et je ne le suis pas" (222).

The old imperatives to find truth and to fix it in the language of a vision recounted, though rejected as delusions at the beginning of this text, return in the boastful pronouncements about the narrator's genius: "Je vais dévoiler tous les mystères: mystères religieux, ou naturels, mort, naissance, avenir, passé, cosmogonie, néant. Je suis maître en fantasmagories. / Ecoutez! ... " (221). Any claim that the statements are ultimately serious is undercut, however, as the rantings of a still delirious narrator, suffering through the night of hell: "Bah! faisons toutes les grimaces imaginables" (222). However, elliptically, the conclusion to the text proposes that interpretation of the present be the condition for return to life; as already established, the process of interpretation engages a subject which lacks conformity to itself and must be scrutinized in its monstrous de-formation: "Ah! remonter à la vie! Jeter les yeux sur nos difformités" (222).

As I have noted above, the interpretive act will increasingly distance itself from the conventions of confession narratives, but it first exhausts that mode in a delirium of confession in the two poems entitled "Délires"; "Vierge folle" and "Alchimie du verbe." In important ways the texts are informative not only for the content of the confessions, a bitterly ironic leave-taking from the old loves ("Vierge folle") and the old modernist poetics ("Alchimie du verbe"), but also as exercises in unlearning certain classical practices of reading: *dé-lire*.[15] What is at stake here is the possibility of a demystified reading of existing literature and of the erotic couple. The act of perversion is itself subject to scrutiny, as mystification, whether it corrupts the esthetics of classical literature, or in a more conventional sexual sense, corrupts the stability of the heterosexual couple by substituting the homosexual couple. The interpretation of these perversions set forth in these two texts ironically reveals the delusions reproduced in the provisional solution.

I will not comment extensively on these two texts, since their pertinence to the problematic I am discussing can be summarized briefly. The two stories recounted in "Délires" are two homologous aspects of the same enterprise: to displace libidinal activity, love or writing, from the determined limits of cultural convention. As Felman has observed, Rimbaud's originality is in conceiving modernity in terms of the couple and in linking desire and language.[16] The enterprise of perversion, of deviation and detour from the beaten path ("les chemins d'ici") bears as well upon the body as upon language. Both are charged with erotic energy which is released through the systematic infraction of interdictions.[17] The contiguity of these two texts unmistakably underscores the interrelation between not dissimilar modes of sexual activity; language is apprehended in its erotic materiality and the production of desire viewed in terms of the operations of language.

"Vierge folle" recounts the perversion of the heterosexual couple, in which its bonds to material productivity are denounced as a domestication of erotic energy. The narrator's utopian sexual ethic is retold by a former companion in hell:

"Il dit: 'Je n'aime pas les femmes. L'amour est à réinventer on le sait. Elles ne peuvent plus que vouloir une position assurée. La position gagnée, coeur et beauté sont mis de côté il ne reste que froid dédain, l'aliment du mariage, aujourd'hui.' " (224)

The problem, as the text will reveal with bitter irony, is not that the narrator misapprehended in the past the deficiencies of the heterosexual couple, and its necessary relation to the dominant culture, but that he reinstated the same suspect imaginary relationship in the homosexual couple.[18] Again in the reported speech of the narrator:

"Tu vois cet élégant jeune homme, entrant dans la belle et calme maison: il s'appelle Duval, Dufour, Armand, Maurice, que sais-je? Une femme est dévouée à aimer ce méchant idiot: elle est morte, c'est certes une sainte au ciel, à présent. Tu me feras mourir comme il a fait mourir cette femme."

(226–7)

The object of the irony here is not only the narrator's companion, but the narrator as well; as the terse final comment by the narrator makes clear: "Drôle de ménage."

The effort to displace the limits of language and to redefine writing takes two forms explicitly in "Alchimie du verbe," and, implicitly, a third, which relates to the problematic status of the writing subject in the present. First, literature is subverted by practices derived from sub-genres excluded from "serious" writing:

A moi, L'histoire d'une de mes folies.

Depuis longtemps, je me vantais de posséder tous les paysages possibles, et trouvais dérisoire les célébrités de la peinture et de la poésie moderne.

J'aimais les peintures idiotes, dessus de portes, décors, toiles de saltim-banques, enseignes, enluminures populaires; la littérature démodée, latin d'église, livres érotiques sans orthographe, romans de nos aieules, contes de fées, petits livres de l'enfance, opéras vieux, refrains niais, rythmes naifs. (228)

The new writing of the recent past displaced the hierarchical distinctions which are the esthetic bases of literary genres, in favor of the excluded or marginal genres. Second, is the claim to have invented a new language which would effectively overcome not only the arbitrary relation between signifier and signified, that very difference which makes meaning possible, but would also conflate the referent with the sign: "J'inventai la couleur des voyelles! . . . je me flattai d'inventer une verbe poétique accessible, un jour ou l'autre, à tous les sens. Je réservais la traduction" (228). Beyond the subversion of traditional literary language, however, and in a manner congruous to that in "Vierge folle," the poet here displaces the conventions of the old literature only to find certain key presuppositions relocated in the new language. The paradox here is that the invention of a radical newness is condemned to repeat the delusions of the past. The mystification which persists is the assumption that literature functions to communicate a fully

retrievable meaning, available to the writing subject and susceptible to appropriation by another subject. In the poetics of the old
"new" literature the narrator simply reinstates the deluded relation
of the subject to language within the same circuit of exchange. The
poet's refusal to "translate" in no way disrupts the underlying
assumptions of the practice; it magnifies the claim to a power of
control attributed to the author of the text. The writer who would
be master of his own fiction in all this *author*ity, inevitably becomes
its dupe. Although elliptically, the final statement of the text
acknowledges that mystification: "Cela s'est passé. Je sais aujourd-
'hui saluer la beauté" (234).

This text marks a break with esthetics in general, whether the
conventions of Literature or of the narrator's former anti-
Literature, and sets up the possibility of significantly different
relation between the writer and writing. We find in this last
sentence of "Alchimie du verbe" an enigmatic echo of the earlier
curse against the muse in the first page of the text ... with the
important difference that denunciation is here replaced with a
respectful salutation. The precise meaning of this address,
however, is impossible to determine, and that may be the most
powerful meaning in this text. The salutation is either a greeting, or
a leave-taking, or both a greeting and a leave-taking. In a sense it
closes the text of delirium, and at the same time turns toward the
possibility of a different understanding of writing. In its undecida-
bility, both a closure and an opening, this last sentence suggests
much about the meaningfulness of the new writing, which will be
both the concentration and the dispersal of sense. The ultimate
folly which this passage deflects is to assume that the writer can ever
greet the muse without at the same time taking leave of his senses.

The predominant importance of *histoire* in these two texts
produces two effects. The first underscores the break between the
subject of this *histoire* and the narrating subject, conveyed most
dramatically by the terse conclusion of each text in the present
tense of *discours*. Second, this break prepares a subsequent and
decisive shift in the discursive registers proposed already in the first
three sections of the poem: the following texts will contain fewer
and fewer passages written as *histoire*. What matters to the narrator
in relating the two stories of the past to the present is the
discontinuity of past time with that of the present, the disjunction
between one of the poet's "other lives," and the present time of
narration. The text thus rejects any reflection upon the possible
continuity between the two subjects of the poem, the subject of the

histoire and the narrating subject. The function of that lacuna is to produce an unbridgeable space between the two instances of the subject.

The four much briefer texts which follow reveal that the narrator desires complete difference between then and now in order that the present self will emerge into a moment which is pure, continuous and uncontaminated by the past. These remaining pages, however, will establish the impossibility of complete separation from the past, and will scrutinize the utopian desire for unalienated presence in *discours*, as past errors are repeated in the present. The desire for an original and non-repetitive modernity, as Felman has remarked, is itself doomed to the form and paradox of repetition.[19] The radical difference in the narrator's awareness before and after "Délires" is the discovery that the break with the past is never definitive, and that the very act of speaking in the present commits the subject to the alienating structures of language, whether that alienation be affirmed or denied.

A first and powerful discovery is that it is impossible to locate the quest outside of the enclosure of Western thought; in short, there is no outside. Earlier, in "Mauvais Sang," the narrator had situated his quest for origins firmly within the metaphoric opposition "inside/outside," simply reversing the polarities and setting the self in an "outside" to which accrues the value of centrality characteristic of the rejected "inside." Here, the issue is treated in a far more complex manner. "M'étant retrouvé deux sous de raison – ça passe vite! – je vois que mes malaises viennent de ne m'être pas figuré assez tôt que nous sommes à l'Occident. Les marais occidentaux!" (235). The expression *se figurer*, beyond its conventional sense meaning "to imagine" or "to understand," suggests a close link with the realization proposed and the acknowledgment that the self can take its "place" only in the figures, the language of the West. Like the discovery that one can never definitively say goodbye to the muse, never leave the realm of figuration, or write a text which does not bear the traces of other texts, this understanding must be set against the earlier assertion that the poet was "intact." Here the narrator abandons claim to an impossible unique and original relation to language and acknowledges that his understanding is mediated by language, which has its laws and configurations which pre-exist the individual and exceed his control.

There simply is no sense in supposing that the narrator can establish a position outside the language and the thought of the

West. The dream of the absolute other, whose metaphoric vehicle in this text is the Orient, is the epitome of self-delusion:

"Les philosophes: Le monde n'a pas d'âge. L'humanité se déplace, simplement. Vous êtes en Occident, mais libre d'habiter dans votre Orient, quelque ancien qu'il vous le faille, – et d'y habiter bien. Ne soyez pas un vaincu. Philosophes, vous êtes de votre Occident." (236)

This awareness is perhaps the most significant gain proposed in "L'Impossible," for it is at this point that the desire for the unique, for the center, can be articulated in the language of discourse, in the recognition that language is powerless to provide the sought-for guarantee of presence. The narrator now begins to think the desire for center in terms of decentering, of displacement of the subject by the language in which it is articulated. This is the point at which it becomes necessary to consider explicitly the limits of language and to affirm at the same time, the self as a configuration of language: "je ne puis pas plus m'expliquer que le mendiant avec ses continuels *Pater* et *Ave Maria. Je ne sais plus parler*" (239). The poet is speechless, confounded, for the language available to him already undercuts his enterprise. It is as corrupt as the language of prayer employed in ludicrous futility by the beggar. This recognition occurs at a highly significant moment in the text, for it is the last statement preceding the pronouncement that the narrator has finished recounting his season in hell: "Pourtant, aujourd-'hui je crois avoir fini la relation de mon enfer." That season is concluded when the narrator has worked out the inadequacies of the historical narrative, but the text does not end in silence, nor does it stop here. Leaving the past seasons "definitively," the narrator turns to the present and "absolute modernity," and the effort to locate the subject in a language totally contemporary to the self.

These sequences in "Adieu," the last section of the text, which repeat the rejected delusions of the past, bring memories into the language of the present: "Je me revois la peau rongée par la boue et la peste, . . . " "L'affreuse évocation" (240). This absorption of the past by the present, completed in "Adieu," permits the poet to dismiss any relation of genetic continuity between the earlier narrated self and the self of the present narration. The moment of the present is the moment to get on with it: "Et allons" (241). Stating things as they are, however, does not mark a moment of epistemological enlightenment, resulting from the appropriation of the past. The imperative here is specified as a desire to forget, and it is the act of forgetting which is burdened with rendering the poet absolutely contemporary:

"Car je puis dire que la victoire m'est acquise: les grincements de dents, les sifflements de feu, les soupirs empestés se modèrent. Tous les souvenirs immondes s'effacent. Mes derniers regrets détalent ... / Il faut être absolument moderne." (241)

Modernity, in the very absoluteness of the desire to be modern, repeats the delusions of the past. "Adieu," as already established in "Alchimie du verbe," where it is articulated with an iterative verb, is never definitive: "Je disais adieu au monde ..." Paradoxically, the status of the modern can never be defined as absolute, for it is inevitably historical and relative, always in a differential relationship to something else.

The poet has acknowledged the divorce between literature, reality and truth: "J'ai cru acquérir des pouvoirs surnaturels. Eh bien! je dois enterrer mon imagination et mes souvenirs! Une belle gloire d'artiste et de conteur emportée!" (240). Following the imperative to be absolutely modern, the rejection of poetry is once again linked to renunciation of its logocentric telos: "Point de cantiques: tenir le pas gagné." This refusal of poetry, significantly, produces ... more poetry: "Et à l'aurore, armés d'une ardente patience, nous entrerons aux splendides villes," and the final words of the poem: "il me sera loisible *de posséder la vérité dans une âme et un corps*" (341). What is perhaps so striking about this conclusion is that it repeats a desire for truth and being in a *structure* of deferral, which is to say, set in the configurations of an impossibility. The text thus does not close upon a moment of presence attained, or even in the confident assertion of a future to be gained, but articulates desire in a structure of difference and displacement. The narrator does not say: "I possess truth in a body and soul," or even "I will possess truth, etc ... " but instead, abandons both the present tense of assertion and the first person subject. Desire is formulated in impersonal language; the integral acting subject has been displaced by the pronoun *il* and the first person has become its object. The reader is left to consider the implication of this confident assertion in which the agent of desire disappears as a first person subject and gives over the subjective function to the "non-person" *il*, and in which the object of desire can only be attained by the narration of a new story, which in turn ...

5

FALSE CONFUSIONS: FICTIONS OF MASCULINE DESIRE IN MALLARMÉ'S "L'APRÈS-MIDI D'UN FAUNE"

Mais, bast! arcane tel élut pour confident
Le jonc vaste et jumeau dont sous l'azur on joue,
Rêve dans un solo long, que nous amusions
La beauté d'alentour par des confusions
Fausses entre elle-même et notre chant crédule; . . .

"L'Après-midi d'un faune" (51)[1]

Un tourbillon de raisons naives ou neuves émane, qu'il plairait de saisir avec sureté: . . .   "Mimique" (310)

What are some of the "false confusions" of Mallarmé's "L'Après-midi d'un faune"? The narrating "voice" of this text seeks to perpetuate a "true" past experience of fulfilled erotic pleasure, yet from the first words of the poem the effort becomes engaged in entanglements of memory, dream and invention. The "true" past recedes in a proliferation of abstractions which ruins the concept of origin in the anticipation of its reconstruction. A major perplexity of the text, initially at least, for the narrator and the reader is to determine *what* is being confused and by *whom*. These questions are "resolved" only when they are understood by the reader, if not the narrator, to be false confusions, for the story narrated and the fictions of desire were and always are confused.

What is the role of narrative in "L'Après-midi . . . "? Is there a story at all in this text, *l'anecdote nécessaire* of which Mallarmé writes in a comment about an early version of the poem?[2] Does the fiction produce a narrated sequence of "events" marked as real, as dream or as fantasy, told by a "voice," the figure of a subject which assumes authority in one way or another for what is being recounted? This chapter will trace some of the entanglements of the faun's "false confusions" about desire, art and interpretation in the complex tensions between the faun's narrative and the fictions of the text.

False confusions

In the second passage quoted from "Mimique," the metaphor *un tourbillon de raisons naives ou neuves* and the conditional expression "qu'il plairait de saisir" suggest that any writing, including that which stages a demystification of naive reasons, also defers the moment of interpretive control. The pleasure of knowing is intimately linked to a modality which displaces the time when things come within our grasp. In the text which follows it is not my desire to substitute for the faun's naive confusions a new and truthful text of disabused interpretation ("qu'il plairait de saisir avec sureté"), but to show how, by displacing and redefining questions about desire, art and interpretation, writing leaves them suspended, pleasurably unresolved.[3] This reading attempts to displace the contexts in which "L'Après-midi . . . " is generally considered. The text is neither simply one of the last poems of Mallarmé's early, still lyric manner, nor already one of the absolutely impersonal texts of the later years. Critics who read the text as a mature form of an impressionist esthetic generally sustain their interpretations by citing the early poems, and the somewhat naive assertions about lyricism and death in the letters written during the crisis of 1864–6. The startling impersonality of this text is thus reabsorbed into a subjectivist, impressionistic esthetics and the events of biography.[4] Others, who emphasize the radical impersonality of the poem, construct their interpretations by advancing an intertext which includes the later essays, particularly "Crise de vers" and "La Musique et les lettres," and the later sonnets.[5] This chapter, on the other hand, assumes that "L'Après-midi . . . " can be considered as a conflictual space, neither entirely cut free from the figures and desires of subjective poetry nor ultimately impersonal in the manner of the late sonnets or of the "pure work" affirmed in "Crise de vers," and other late theoretical writings. Specular desire, reflexive thought and rhetorical forms necessary to sustain them are destroyed in the articulations of the text, but not without residue. These are some of the tensions and dis-appearances which I will trace here.

While threads of narrative and fragments of description occur throughout this poem, they are but the debris of an outmoded practice of fiction which entraps the desiring subject; the writing, however, undoes this specular subject, activating in the intersections of narrative and description another text which marks the dispersal of subjectivity and the proliferation of supplementary desire and interpretation.[6] The poem intricately combines naive assertions of the faun's desire with the complex reflections of a

97

fiction engaged in dismantling the terms in which desire is initially figured. The text thus causes the object(s) it names to disappear by means of a language which, as Blanchot has noted, refuses representations and destroys and annihilates objects.[7] Though he never does sort things out, the faun is an artist and an interpreter, whose musings illuminate certain confusions about the artist-creator. In breaking with certain forms of desire and meaning, the fiction derives its significance from an unstable relation between those forms and its difference. Any reading which might attempt to disengage a stable narrative and thematic structure, to restore a clearly delimited diegetic space or a singular voice, is doomed to repeat errors no less naive, despite their subtlety, than those of the faun. The poem both produces and suspends narrative; it describes and speculates and blurs the distinction between decor and thought; a lyric "voice" "speaks" and thus becomes fragmented and depersonalized. An allegory of desire and esthetic production, the poem allegorizes its own production of meaning without ever achieving a totalizing, transfiguring moment; it is a deferring of intentionality and interpretation.

In a sense, then, "L'Après-midi d'un faune" is the same old story, an archaically decorative allegory with a descendent of Pan as its central figure. The text re-enacts a scene of masculine desire according to a familiar and seemingly secure libidinal economy. With naive aggressiveness, the faun attempts to order desire according to dichotomous articulations between an active, masculine subject and passive, feminine objects, and to place the participants in narrative and description in ways which perpetuate the hierarchy of active subject and passive object. These roles are distributed here as: to see / be seen; to violate / be violated; to know / be known; to tell / be told.[8] The wish to possess and retain in verbal and sexual reproduction is entrusted with authenticating the desiring subject as a conscious presence, whose individual and privileged viewpoint is capable of retrieving in the other its own origins:

> Allors m'éveillerai-je à la ferveur première,
> Droit et seul, sous un flot antique de lumière ...

The projected possession of the nymphs by the faun's erotic regard is charged with assuming mastery as subject, yet as we shall see, these efforts to locate an accessible other result only in a specular mirroring of masculine desire which is ultimately ruined by the fiction.

False confusions

A will to appropriate feminine presence is asserted confidently, and with a certain vanity in the first words of the text:

Ces nymphes, je les veux perpétuer.

Of course, the narrator immediately becomes involved in interpreting what may or may not have taken place:

Aimai-je un rêve?

Further on in the opening lines of the poem, the speculations turn toward disentangling a hypothetical, fantasmatic projection:

Réfléchissons . . .
ou si les femmes dont tu gloses
Figurent un souhait de tes sens fabuleux!

Dream, reflection, interpretation, extraordinarily intense desire ("tes sens fabuleux") and the meanings produced by the maker of fables (if one reads *tes sens fabuleux* in another way), however diverse and unstable they may be ultimately in the fiction, are brought together initially around the faun's wish to possess, to tell and to interpret.

One reading of the text must account for this telos and the rhetorical conventions which converge with it to sustain a specular relationship between a desiring subject and what is called upon to reflect it, an elusive feminine presence, whose deferral gives substance and dimension to masculine desire:

O nymphes, regonflons des SOUVENIRS divers

Those "memories" are diversely reflected as a story of a past encounter, a dream or projected fantasy and the faun's theories of what may or may not have been. Description, representation and the efforts to fix the identity of objects of desire are inextricably intertwined. Following the faun's deluded strategies, let us consider them initially at least as though they were distinct, in the hope that the impasses we encounter will help to locate elsewhere the shifts and distortions of meaning. Let us first examine the faun's attempts to name and reconstruct in description what he desired, and then consider how description is called upon to define and authenticate the still elusive objects of desire.

In one sense the false confusions of the passage read at the beginning of this chapter are generated by a desire which conflates its own song ("notre chant crédule") with the desired beauty ("la beauté d'alentour"). At least a double metonymy, the latter expression figures in a tantalizing ambiguity both the nymphs and the decor. It suggests that the faun's credulity lies, at least to some degree, in the attempt to reduce the already multiple, diverse and fragmentary ("ces nymphes ... les femmes dont tu gloses") to a singular, personified object: "la beauté d'alentour." The quest for the feminine, as we shall see later, not only seeks unity where there is multiplicity and difference, but cannot maintain distinctions between a desired feminine presence and the decor which is called upon to reflect it.

The faun's speculations further on in the poem assert both that he ravished the nymphs together without disentangling them, although they were two, and that it was a crime to divide what had been so well *con*fused:

> *J'accours; quand, à mes pieds, s'entrejoignent (meurtries*
> *De la langueur goûtée à ce mal d'être deux)*
> *Des dormeuses parmi leurs seuls bras hasardeux;*
> *Je les ravis, sans les désenlacer, et vole*
> *A ce massif, hai par l'ombrage frivole, ...*

The fault, it is said, is to have divided the couple:

> *Mon crime, c'est d'avoir, gai de vaincre ces peurs*
> *Traitresses, divisé la touffe échevelée*
> *De baisers que les dieux gardaient si bien mêlée:*
> *Car, à peine j'allais cacher un rire ardent*
> *Sous les replis heureux d'une seule (gardant*
> *Par un doigt simple, afin que sa candeur de plume*
> *Se teignît à l'émoi de sa soeur qui s'allume,*
> *La petite, naive et ne rougissant pas:) ...*

More is lost in these two passages than a presence which may or may not have been. Not only is the desired unity already multiple, but feminine arousal takes place elsewhere than where the faun wished to locate it. The other's pleasure is an interruption of the account of masculine desire; in effect, it cannot be accounted for in the economy of his desire. There is no *place* in this discourse for the feminine as "object," whether we interpret it as fictionally "real" and lost, or as fantasmatic. There is a crucial slippage here between the meaning articulated by the fictional voice ("Mon crime, c'est ...") and that produced by the writing, which points both to the investment placed in narrative and to its failures. Narrative is charged with making the meaning of loss accessible to the subject; it is a strategy to regain an impossible unity, anterior to difference.[9]

In each passage, a parenthesis breaks the faun's discourse and inscribes a feminine pleasure indifferent and supplementary to the account which the male attempts to formulate. In the first passage:

> *(meurtries*
> *De la langueur goûtée à ce mal d'être deux)*

and in the second

> *(gardant*
> *Par un doigt simple, afin que sa candeur de plume*
> *Se teignît à l'émoi de sa sœur qui s'allume,*
> *La petite, naive et ne rougissant pas:)*

Feminine erotic activity literally takes place in a gap in the narrator's discourse, between two feminine figures. Excluded in the unattainable specificity of its otherness, feminine pleasure surfaces as an interruption of syntax, which suspends and short-circuits the faun's tale.

Whether one reads the expression *émoi* as "agitation" or, following more problematic resonances, as *et moi*, which would suggest that the active sister of the couple is a double of the faun, this erotic moment produces a space which excludes a certain figure of sexuality and disrupts the polarities of masculine and feminine, active and passive. To what agent is the single finger ("un doigt simple . . . ") linked metonymically? The present participle *gardant* requires us to associate that gesture not only with the faun, but with one of the nymphs. A further consequence of this parenthetic interruption is to force a passive role upon the faun, as the last three verses of this passage indicate:

> *Car, à peine j'allais cacher un rire ardent*
> *Sous les replis heureux d'une seule (gardant*
> *Par un doigt simple, afin que sa candeur de plume*
> *Se teignît à l'émoi de sa soeur que s'allume,*
> *La petite, naive et ne rougissant pas:)*
> *Que de mes bras, défaits par de vagues trépas,*
> *Cette proie, à jamais ingrate se délivre*
> *Sans pitié du sanglot dont j'étais encore ivre.*

The exchange not only plays itself out as a break in the story, but to the extent that we can find a "masculine" intrusion in the space of this parenthesis, it is impossible to point with any certainty to an agent which can be identified as masculine or feminine according to the faun's schema of things. "Masculinity" and "femininity" divide and multiply sexuality from within.

Other complex associations linked to the expression *la beauté d'al-entour* concern the function of the decor in this poem. The faun has invoked the decor to give meaning to the story which seeks formulation; it is called upon as witness to the "events" and, obliquely, tacitly, to validate this account of desire in a long tradition:

> O bords siciliens d'un calme marécage
> Qu'à l'envie de soleils ma vanité saccage,
> Tacite sous les fleurs d'etincelles, CONTEZ

By using the figure of personification and exhorting the setting to represent what was "real," this naive imperative relies upon conventional artifice at the very moment when rhetoric should be effaced. Where one anticipates that the description of the decor would serve as a "reality effect"[10] to occult implicitly the rhetorical status of language, the text engages a figure to speak the truth of its non-figural status. The poem plays here with pre-suppositions traditionally associated with descriptive passages in literature. Description pre-supposes a knowledge about things and words which can be considered as a generalized cultural text, a catalog of lexical items appropriate to the terms elaborated in the passage (here, the terms are *bords siciliens*). Description thus produces an *effet de vérité* by neutralizing textual operations and passing itself off as a relation between words and things, rather than as a selective repetition of elements of an anterior text, a culturally determined inventory.[11] The faun, as both a teller and an interpreter of description lacks the knowledge pre-supposed as necessary to descriptive texts; he does not recognize the already known, nor does he learn from the decor what he does not know. Description is called upon here, implicitly, to serve as a truth effect, but also more directly, and carrying that rhetorical effect to its farthest limit in a juridical and argumentative sense, it is called upon to serve as *witness*.[12] The insistence with which this passage exposes the threadbare artifices of literature suggests how radically different Mallarmé's poetic language is from the conventions of subjective expression and descriptive representation to which this poem alludes. This passage engages a problematics which Mallarmé explores in many of the most important theoretical writings; the necessary distinction between poetic language and the language of representation:

Abolie, la prétention, esthétiquement une erreur, quoi-qu'elle régît les chefs-d'oeuvre, d'inclure au papier subtil du volume autre chose que par exemple l'horreur de la forêt, ou le tonnerre muet épars au feuillage; non le bois intrinsèque et dense des arbres.   "Crise de vers" (365–6)

This is not a formula for impressionism, as though the poet wishes to "paint" nature and to establish a congruence between objects and language. Mallarmé's explorations, the failed project of the faun, or the affirmations of the critical texts, clear the way for the emergence of a radically different language, which accounts for Nature through "transpositions" in terms distinct from "cette fonction de numéraire facile et représentatif" (368). Fictions take place alongside Nature, they neither represent nor replace it:

La Nature a lieu, on n'y ajoutera pas, que des cités, les voies ferrées et plusieurs inventions formant notre materiel.

Tout l'acte disponible, à jamais et seulement, reste de saisir les rapports, entre temps, rares ou multipliés; d'après quelque état intérieur et que l'on veuille à son gré entendre, simplifier le monde.

"La Musique et les lettres" (647)

Writing and nature are absolutely distinct; fiction produces relations of significance in a lack which "is" consciousness: "A l'égal de créer: la notion d'un object, échappant qui fait défaut" (647). Writing is produced, as Mallarmé suggests in "La Musique et les lettres," by the lack of coincidence between consciousness and Nature (and anything beyond), and the consciousness of that lack: "le conscient manque chez nous de ce qui là-haut éclate" (647). "L'Après-midi . . . " traces the work of negativity which liberates us from things, as Blanchot remarks: "C'est donc ce manque, ce vide, cet espace vacant qui est l'objet et la création propre du langage."[13]

Just as description in the passage we have been considering blurs the distinctions it was called upon to validate, it problematizes features which we rely upon in texts to structure the instance of the person. Italics in this passage might serve to mark the sequence as reported speech, but the subordinating *que*, combined with the imperfect verb tense, suggest rather that this is indirect discourse; the expected shift to the third person ("qu'*il* coupait"), however, never takes place, Strikingly, the first person intrudes just where the third person would provide the evidence that the scene did take place, and that it can be represented by telling. Paradoxically, the first person here erodes the distinction it earlier asserted it sought. Just as a shift in narrative voice might occur, the faun, as narrator, reappears to produce confusions about voice and story.[14]

We have seen how a certain schema of specular desire voiced by the faun has been disrupted and how the wish to know, repeat and appropriate in narrative and to reflect in description has been undone. I would now like to turn to other aspects of this ferment of disintegration by tracing in greater detail the questioning of the opposition between tropes and the proper, the functions of ellipsis and hypothetical modes in narrative and, finally, the deconstruction of the first person pronoun as it is supplemented by other pronominal forms.

In the opening lines of the poem several features of the text link a persona and its voice in the here and now of the enunciation to the assertion of a desire to possess: "Ces nymphes, je les veux perpétuer . . ." Not only the verb *perpétuer*, but the pronouns and the demonstrative *ces*, as deictic features, establish an axis of desire and a context of immediacy. However confidently the statement may be linked to an acting subject, to a present moment and to an implicit future of erotic fulfillment, it is already marked by difference, division and even death. The expression which asserts the will to appropriate resonates with a somber echo: "je les veux perpétuer / perpé*tuer*."[15] This passage may foreshadow the final line of the poem ("Couple, adieu; je vais voir l'ombre que tu devins") and suggest already that the figure which the sleeping faun will seek at the end of the poem is not simply a dream image but a more deathly shadow. Whether or not one reads the opening line as I have suggested, a deflection from the proper is already apparent in the disjunction between the desiring subject and the erotic object, marked syntactically by the disarticulated alexandrine of the first line: "Si clair / Leur incarnat léger, qu'il voltige dans l'air . . ." The erotic object is fragmented by a metonymy ("leur incarnat léger") which then becomes confused with a setting which should frame the scene. This figuration of the objects of desire introduces a series of terms which are grammatically masculine, suggesting that the metonymic fragmentation of the object is part of a more radical disruption of the proper. We have already noted the interruption of masculine "unity" and the deconstruction of oppositions in the parenthetical lines on the nymph's pleasure; the following passage suggests that the play on gender which we have discussed is more than the illogical and arbitrary work of grammar:

> Inerte, tout brûle dans l'heure fauve
> Sans marquer par quel art ensemble détala
> Trop d'hymène souhaité de qui cherche le *la*:
> Alors m'éveillerai-je à la ferveur première,
> Droit et seul, sous un flot antique de lumière,
> *Lys, et l'un de vous tous pour l'ingénuité.*   (italics added)

On one level, of course, the expression "le *la*" refers to the song of the faun's flute, but the reader attuned to the questions we are discussing will explore other implications, here the possible chiasmatic inversions between words which signify directly or figuratively the male or the female sex (*lys*) and their signified. Furthermore, sex literally lacks nominal substance; it is "signified" as an ellipsis of the proper term (le *la* . . .). In a more radical sense, perhaps, sexuality is purely a matter of relations between "shifters" (le *là*), "nothing" but a question of discourse in a context which never fixes differences among missing terms.

Disturbances between figurative and proper in the opening lines extend immediately to the thinking "subject," which is no more present in its own thought than are the nymphs in a "real" decor:

> Aimai-je un rêve?
> Mon doute, amas de nuit ancienne, s'achève
> En maint rameau subtil, qui, demeuré les vrais
> Bois mêmes, prouve, hélas! que bien seul je m'offrais
> Pour triomphe la faute idéale de roses.

The metonymic branching of doubt becomes entangled with the "real woods" in such a way that figural language and what the text signifies as proper commingle and divide, proving in what one critic has called a "*démonstration*" that any thought, even thought which testifies to the truth of its doubt, can only be articulated in the structure of a fiction ("maint rameau subtil").[16] The faun's reasoning collides with what the text alludes to as real, the fictional proper, suggesting that the real is knowable only as the absence of proper meaning. No link is established here between thought and "reality," a referent which would support cognition; instead, the faun's thought rebounds from a "real" already contaminated by figural language, to grasp a solitude and an absence ("la faute idéale de roses"). The relation between reason and what is signified as the material is an unbridgeable gap whose space is augmented here by the use of the language of logic. There is a paradoxical relation here between the faun's narrative, which decries a loss of sense and presence, and the meaning of the fiction, which has located one of the most powerful resources of Mallarmé's writing. The significant gap between language and materiality produces a language of absence and silence, which as Blanchot has noted: "fait appel à quelquechose de matériel, se rend présent d'une manière qui ruine l'orgueilleux édifice élevé sur le vide et lui, l'absence même, n'a pour s'introduire dans le monde des valeurs signifiées et abstraites, d'autres ressources que de se réaliser comme chose."[17]

In what follows, the attempts to distinguish between the "real" nymphs and analogs, a blue spring which weeps and a warm breeze, which may be sources of the vision, or figurative projections, produce infinite regressions away from an absent center. What is located here is not a space, nor bodies, signified as real, but a most moving question in Mallarmé's writing, the question of whether there is occasion (or a place) for writing.[18]

> Réfléchissons ...
>   ou si les femmes dont tu gloses
> Figurent un souhait de tes sens fabuleux!
> Faune, l'illusion s'échappe des yeux bleus
> Et froids, comme une source en pleurs, de la plus chaste:
> Mais, l'autre tout soupirs, dis-tu qu'elle contraste
> Comme brise du jour chaude dans ta toison?

Precisely where the desire to interpret is asserted most forcefully, the separation between the "real" of the fiction and the tropes becomes most problematic ("ou si les femmes dont tu gloses / figurent un souhait de tes sens fabuleux!"). All the terms which description and interpretation seek to separate in order to grasp the real, intermingle and merge finally with fiction-making. The passage sets the scene for the transposition from deluded speculation to writing, that surplus of sense inaccessible to the faun's desire.

The operations of language which make description impossible reinforce a negative relation to the "real"; by denying any such link, the text affirms the intimate similarities between music and letters:

> Mais, l'autre tout soupirs, dis-tu qu'elle contraste
> Comme brise du jour chaude dans ta toison?
> Que non! par l'immobile et lasse pâmoison
> Suffocant de chaleurs le matin frais s'il lutte,
> Ne murmure point d'eau que ne verse ma flûte
> Au bosquet arrosé d'accords; et le seul vent
> Hors des deux tuyaux prompt à s'exhaler avant
> Qu'il disperse le son dans une pluie aride,
> C'est, à l'horizon pas remué d'une ride,
> Le visible et serein souffle artificiel
> De l'inspiration, qui regagne le ciel.

The figures in this passage borrow the motifs of one art (music) to supplement the resources of verbal language; "brise de jour chaude" is negated by the metaphor of the water pouring from the flute; the only wind is that produced by the flute which is figured in another negative metaphor as a dry rain. There is no hierarchy here between the arts, in which language would interpret music or vice versa, but rather a relay and resonance of figural motifs, such that distinctions disappear in a play of similarities and difference: "L'un des modes incline à l'autre et y disparaissant, ressort avec emprunts ..."[19] What the writing has produced, however, the narrator attempts to refuse. In a naively petulant gesture the faun throws away the flute, a treacherous instrument, as unreliable as the decor or the nymphs as a recorder of the scene:

> Tache donc, instrument des fuites, ô maligne
> Syrinx, de refleurir aux lacs où tu m'attends!

Art is musical and not instrumental. Throughout the text, the simultaneous fragmentation and reappearance of objects of desire is accompanied by the interruption and ellipsis of narrative, which frequently re-emerges, transformed, as hypothesis or remains suspended. Mallarmé has described such effects elsewhere in the critical texts where they are not only the subject of analysis but are put in play in the broken syntax and complex rhythms of these texts. In "Crise de vers": "Tout devient suspens, disposition fragmentaire avec alternance et vis-à-vis, concourant au rythme total, lequel serait le poème tu ..." (367) and in the preface to *Un Coup de dès*: "Tout se passe par raccourci, en hypothèse: on évite le récit."[20] Not only are these effects of ellipsis and interruption the subject of intertextual resonances, they are alluded to by the sub-title of the poem: *Eglogue*. Suspended below the title, this sub-title announces the subject of the text as an archaically decorative fantasy, a pastoral poem; it also suggests obliquely how the notions of subject and of completeness are to be suspended. An eclogue is not only a pastoral poem, it is a selection, hence a fragment, of a larger work. The sub-title thus alludes here to an ever-absent total text, of which the poem would be a part; the writing, however, constantly interrupts continuity at every level of discourse, constantly deferring what it demonstrates to be a lure.[21]

Narrative in "L'Après-midi ..." is suspended in so far as it might constitute a coherent chronological sequence determined by apparent or "deep" logical structures; what remains is a rhythmic organization of fragments and hypotheses:

> Réfléchissons ...

This imperative could lead to the connections of either story or theory; instead, a new sequence is introduced after the unbridgeable gap produced by deletion marks and the white space of the page. What follows, then, is neither a continuation nor a new beginning:

> ou si les femmes dont tu gloses . . .

The form of logic remains (" . . . ou si . . . "), though it is hopelessly disarticulated. It is the disabled hypothesis of a feminine presence which lacks the terms necessary to flesh out the supposition. The text shatters the syntactic armature required by narrative discourse.

A passage quoted earlier, in which the faun turns to the watery banks, produces similar effects through ellipsis and hypothesis, which are allegorized here in a typically mallarméen ambiguity as "*ce vol de cygnes* . . .", a flight or theft of swans or of signs:

> *Et qu'au prélude lent où naissent les pipeaux*
> *Ce vol de cygnes, non! de naîades se sauve*
> *Ou plonge* . . .

Even the final lines of the poem, which project the story of a rape of Venus, admittedly an impressive narrative climax, lead to an alternate, supplementary story introduced by "Non, mais . . . " The conjunction *mais*, which at the beginning of a phrase should introduce a logical link to what precedes, is here cut off from that link by the negative *non*, thus cancelling the proleptic narrative of desire. That narrative seemed to foretell a naively "real" moment of possession, in the present ("Je tiens la reine . . . ") in which the divisions of desire are to be fused at last, yet the text is again broken by interruption and ellipsis:

> Etna! c'est parmi toi visité de Vénus
> Sur ta lave posant ses talons ingénus,
> Quand tonne un somme triste ou s'épuise la flamme.
> Je tiens la reine!
>   O sûr châtiment . . .
>   Non, mais l'âme
> De paroles vacante et ce corps alourdi
> Tard succombent au fier silence de midi:

The poem ends with the suspension of the present:

> Couple, adieu; je vais voir l'ombre que tu devins.

The becoming (*devenir*) which the faun will see in the future ("je vais voir") has already elapsed ("que tu devins"). The projected future and the past become entangled, so that time, and consequently narrative, are suspended. The singular personal pronoun *tu* suggests, nevertheless, the possibility that, outside of time and narrative the objects of desire have finally become unified, accessible to the controlling regard in some virtual, undetermined moment. This line is subverted by a negativity, however, which ruins the possibility of this transcendence. *Tu* is not only the other of desire, the present or virtual interlocutor, it is emptiness, silence ("l'âme/De paroles vacante ..."). As the text inscribes the pronoun, however, it silences voice, which paradoxically re-emerges in the vitality and sonorous emptiness of the pronoun.

The fantasmatic shade at the end of the poem ("l'ombre que tu devins") produces an uncanny play of reflections in an illuminating collision of meaning, such as Mallarmé alludes to in a well-known passage of "Crise de vers": "par le heurt de leur inégalité mobilisés; ils [les mots] s'allument de reflets réciproques comme une virtuelle trainée de feux sur des pierreries ..." (365). The same passage from "Crise de vers" and this last line of the poem link these conjunctions, deflections and crystalline shock effects to a particularly mallarméen deconstruction of person and voice, an *elocutionary disappearance:*

L'ocuvre pure implique la disparition élocutoire du poète, qui cède l'initiative aux mots, par le heurt de leur inégalité mobilisés; ils s'allument de reflets réciproques comme une virtuelle trâinée de feux sur des pierreries, remplaçant la respiration perceptible en l'ancien souffle lyrique ou direction personnelle enthousiaste de la phrase.   (366)

Indicators of the person, shifters, are not absent from the poem; they are everywhere, disseminated throughout the text in ways which disarticulate the figure of presence, the "ancient lyric voice." Returning to the final line of the text, one can retrace some of these complex dis-appearances. The final instance of the first person echoes the opening line: "je les veux ... je vais voir ... " This is not a repetition of the same, however, but a mark of discordance with the presumed meaning of the initial pronoun. The first person is associated metonymically throughout the poem with voice, breath and inspiration, and with the flute. The link between these terms is, in one sense, written as though it were linear: "une sonore, vaine et monotone ligne." This noise about vanity suggests once again that insistence on the assertion of desire, self-consciousness and theorizing serves to point out a complex of failure. Vanity is a hyperbolic motif running throughout the text, linked to desire ("O bords siciliens d'un calme marécage/Qu'à l'envie ma vanité saccage ...") and to song or voice ("Moi, de ma rumeur fier, je vais parler longtemps / Des déesses ... "). The insistent voicing of the first person and its metonym, vanity, pridefully asserts a positive motif, the faun's naive confidence, yet it advances, at the same time, another equally insistent sense: vanity as emptiness, absence. Similarly, throughout the text the first person pronoun and other shifters associated with it, possessive adjectives, the *tu* of the *je/tu* dyad and others, enter into complex relations which destabilize the subject and mark its disappearance as a locus of being. The discursive references of the term *je* are so complex that the pronoun cannot stand as a figure of the person in any traditional lyric sense. The *I* of the discourse enters into very unstable combinations with *tu/nous/il* and even *on*. De Man has noted in a very rich analysis that the term "voice" and the pronouns associated with it serve as metaphors by which we infer analogically the intent of the subject by the structure of the predicate.[22] We have seen that the predicate, narrative and description, cannot represent or otherwise sustain the subject. On another level, furthermore, the interplay of pronouns undoes the discursive reference which shifters require, according to Benveniste's well-known schema, and which is the basis of the relations between *je* and *tu* fundamental to lyric poetry.[23] Specifically, the *je/tu* axis is shattered, as is the anticipated relation between these instances of the person and the non-person *il*. The first person is supplemented by *nous*; the singular is first doubled by *tu* and redoubled by *nous*, producing an irreducible excess of "person," which, as desire and passion, is eccentric to itself:

> Tu sais ma passion, que, pourpre et déjà mure,
> Chaque grenade éclate et d'abeilles murmure;
> Et notre sang, épris de qui le va saisir,
> Coule pour tout l'essaim éternel du désir.

In a passage quoted earlier, *I* comes to occupy the place of the interlocutor and cannot be restored to any proper place. In the lines beginning "Réfléchissons ... " the second person only functions to maintain the possibility of discourse while blurring the positions of expressive exchange, making way for the impersonal voices of the poem. The plural *réfléchissons* includes both the split person of interior monolog ("ou si les femmes dont tu gloses ... ", "dis-tu qu'elle contraste ... ") and the virtual second person interlocutor, the nymphs. In these opening lines, reflection is not the effect of a simple specular mirroring of consciousness, but a potentially limitless interplay of reciprocal reflection. Supplementary "identities" in this text further extend to the third person, as the relative pronoun *qui* indicates in these lines:

> Inerte tout brûle dans l'heure fauve
> Sans marquer par quel art ensemble détala
> Trop d'hymen souhaité de qui cherche le *la* . . .

The flute player is even designated by the indefinite third person *on. I* is another:

> Le jonc vaste et jumeau dont sous l'azur on joue . . .

Mallarmé first mentions the poem which was to become "L'Après-midi d'un faune" in letters to Cazalis in 1865, in which he speaks of an early dramatic version, an act in verse: "Monologue d'un faune," intended to be recited on stage by an actor. The letters indicate that all the terms we have been considering (subject/object, story, setting, etc.) which are posed initially and effaced in "L'Après-midi . . . " remained, in the earlier version, intact:

> je rime un intermède héroïque, dont le héros est un Faune. Ce poème renferme une très haute et belle idée, mais les vers sont terriblement difficiles à faire, car je le fais absolument scénique, non possible au théâtre, mais exigeant le théâtre. Et cependant, je veux conserver toute la poésie de mes oeuvres lyriques, mon vers même, que j'adapte au drame. (1449)

Although Banville and others had made the dramatic monologue popular at the time, Mallarmé's piece was not accepted, lacking, as the poet comments ironically in another letter, the anecdote necessary to please the public:

> Les vers de mon *Faune* ont plu infiniment, mais de Banville et Coquelin n'y ont pas rencontré l'anecdote nécessaire que demande le public et m'ont affirmé que cela n'intéresserait que les poètes. (1450)

Mallarmé's later version of the poem dramatizes what is implicit in the necessity for anecdote and the terms which sustain narrative. Obliquely, or according to popular etymology, ob-scenely, what is played out in "L'Après-midi . . . " is the death of the subject voice and story and the dis-appearances which produce other scenes, other desires.

The death of the poet as an expressive self in Mallarmé's fictions has been well documented; there is little interest in reiterating here what has been so convincingly demonstrated elsewhere.[24] If, however, the absence of identity makes way for differences other than those hierarchical and oppositional sorts examined at the

111

beginning of this chapter, we may have reason to turn once again to the problem of the subject and to what might be understood by an "elocutionary disappearance." It is not sufficient to remark that the faun and his double, the poet, are effaced by the text. The expression *la disparition élocutoire* suggests not only that the text nullifies the ancient lyric breath and the scene to which it gives voice, but that absence is produced *through* elocutionary effects, writing or speech. Lyrical eloquence is silenced, but there are material traces of consciousness which are neither expressive nor subjective, no longer anchored in the first person pronoun ("dont le héros est un Faune . . . ") nor bound by the *je/tu* dyade of the "old" lyric. While these terms are not dismissed from Mallarmé's poem and remain scattered in the fiction as privileged nostalgic centers, they are everywhere supplemented by other pronominal forms which deflect a return of the narcissistic ego and its specular supports. Consciousness is affirmed without "being present."

"L'Après-midi . . . " proliferates traces of subjectivity in a dispersal which interrupts the fictions of identity. By dismantling the opposition between subject and object and by tilting the fragile equilibrium which would sustain the subject in control of the other(s) and its other, the text affirms shifting division of consciousness. A paragraph of the essay "La Musique et les lettres" (1894) proposes a relationship between writing and desire not unlike that worked out by the destruction of representation and the specular subject in "L'Après-midi . . . "

Avec véractié, qu'est-ce, les Lettres, que cette mentale poursuite, menée, en tant que le discours, afin de définir ou de faire, à l'égard de soi-même, preuve que le spectacle répond à une imaginative compréhension, il est vrai, dans l'espoir de s'y mirer. (648)

The text offers the "hope" of an imaginary comprehension of a "spectacle" in excess of the specular relations of the Imaginary.[25] That is the text as desire and celebration of the consciousness of fiction.

The verb *mirer*, used here in the absolute, impersonal infinitive, engages a complex of reflections already set in play by "L'Après-midi d'un faune," displacing the "false confusions" of certain relations in fiction. *S'y mirer*: the verb opens up shifting, glancing relays which cannot be fixed in the order of a *mis-en-abyme*, nor be delimited by the grammar and logic of the reflexive. *Y* is anaphoric to *une imaginative compréhension*, *le spectacle*, *soi-même*, *le discours*, *cette mentale poursuite*, *les Lettres*, or to any one or combination of these terms according to syntactic choices, all possible, and meaningful. *Mirer*, from popular Latin *mirare*, "to look at attentively"; "to candle an egg by holding it to the light"; "to take aim with a gun"; figurative: *mirer une place* . . . "to aspire to a position." In its pronominal form: "to look at oneself in a mirror or at another object which relays the image of oneself"; figuratively: "see oneself," "recognize oneself," "to take pleasure, to delight in, to revel in someone or something."

6

THE TRIALS OF AUTHORITY UNDER LOUIS BONAPARTE

The texts which I have discussed in the preceding pages were written in a relatively brief moment, roughly from 1848 to 1875, punctuated by two major revolutions (June, 1848, and the Paris Commune of 1871), which failed to deflect the consolidation of bourgeois political and cultural hegemony.[1] It may be assumed that the uncanny textual similarities of these writings, associated as they always are with the decentering and fragmentation of the subject and with the disruption of hierarchical relations (prose/poetry, narrator/protagonist, masculine/feminine, etc.), are related also to instabilities in the wider social order, in the symbolic representations of power. A brief parallel reading of texts whose apparent differences need hardly be emphasized, Marx's well-known essays on Napoléon III and the beginnings of the Second Empire, *The Class Struggles in France: 1848–1850* and *The 18th Brumaire of Louis Bonaparte*, and the documents of Flaubert's and Baudelaire's trials in 1857 for "offenses to public morality," will outline connections between specific symbolic operations in the sociopolitical order and the writing practices which I have discussed.[2] In the pages that follow, I am not seeking to establish relations of historical determinism, an expressive causality,[3] between the historical and literary text, but to trace the configurations of certain fissures in the symbolic system of political representation which have powerful structural affinities with those disruptions of subjectivity and narrative in the literary texts I have discussed. I will examine a conjunction between discursive registers, the literary and the historical, in the formation and representation of authority, and the defense through censorship of its key institutions, the church, the family and conventional esthetic forms. This inquiry into the complex interaction between the political, ideological and fictional is hypothetical and exploratory and not intended to establish determinate lines of causality; indeed, such a theoretical narrative would be inimical to my project in this book. This last

114

chapter is undertaken in the conviction that questions explored earlier in the book necessarily lead to those broader issues which concern the intertwining between history and fiction.

Within the practices of bourgeois art, within what Althusser has called the ideological apparatus of the state, the texts of Baudelaire, Flaubert, Rimbaud and Mallarmé, as I have shown, constantly give form to the contradictions rending the political and social edifice.[4] They strike at the base of the enabling authority of ideology, the subject, and at the very stability of narrative form, which is required to articulate the representations of order. My speculative examination of a certain disequilibrium in the discourse of political power, those fictions by which power establishes and sustains itself, will prepare the ground for a clearer understanding of the ways in which the literary texts I have read struggle with the dominant which inhabits them.[5] What follows, then, attempts to open up the inquiry onto those wider and complex questions of how literary texts both reproduce the political unconscious of their time and provide very powerful forms of symbolic resistance to the dominant. The context will now include the social order in a broader analysis of discourse: those symbolic messages "transmitted to us by the co-existence of various sign systems" within a cultural context that includes both the literary and the political.[6]

The initial conjunction between the writings discussed above and Marx's texts on the second Napoleonic period can be made in terms of this observation in the opening pages of *The 18th Brumaire of Louis Bonaparte*:

Men make their own history, but they do not make it just as they please; they do not make it under the circumstances chosen by themselves, but under circumstances directly encountered, given and transmitted from the past.[7]

Marx describes the movement of history in a backward glance, claiming that men represent their own present circumstances by repeating the figures, the narratives and the language of the past:

And just when they seem engaged in revolutionizing themselves and things, in creating something that has never yet existed, precisely in such periods of revolutionary crisis they anxiously conjure up the spirits of the past to their service and borrow from them names, battle-cries and costumes in order to present the new scene of world history in this time-honored disguise and this borrowed language.[8]

The "subject," in short, never inhabits "his own" language and is constantly engaged in recalling from the past figures which make it

115

possible to assume subjectivity. He repeats the forms of the past, while producing the forms of the present. For Marx, the specificity of nineteenth-century revolutions, unlike earlier revolutions, is that they should look forward and not backward. He states the problem in terms of an imperative to invent a new language, much as the authors I have discussed struggle with the implications of their own writing practices and the manifest incongruities between their texts and the still vital forms of the past: "There the words went beyond the content; here the content goes beyond the words."[9] Marx's own system, however different from that he condemns, bears the mark of its time. In the historical misrepresentation which Marx questions, the past is seen as a moment of origin charged with remedying the dilemma of a subject dislodged from effective presence in the here and now, heterogeneous to history. Marx, however, in turning the schema around, and projecting that origin upon the future, like the narrator of Rimbaud's *Une Saison en enfer*, refuses to repeat the figures and narratives of the past and opens up the possibility of producing new forms of subjectivity and different narratives for action.[10]

The active subject of history and the narrative of history can only be misunderstood as deformed repetition. Marx, in *The 18th Brumaire*, *The Class Struggles in France*, and Sartre in *L'Idiot de la famille*, have insisted on the comic travesty of authority which sustained imperial rule; "False nephew, phony emperor, phony war, phony court, phony aristocrats."[11] As Mehlman has shown, Marx's writings on the years from 1848 to 1852 make repeated and damaging reference to the Napoleonic rule as rhetorical repetition, a degraded form of drama; not tragedy, but farce.[12] Consolidation of the power of the bourgeoisie thus relied on mis-representations masking fundamental contradictions which ultimately turned its order against itself.[13] The farce of repetition in the case of the second Napoléon is a radical and scandalous break with the *episteme* of representation.[14] For Marx, the failure of representation is both a source of laughter and derision, figured in the remark about history as farce and disseminated throughout his texts in terms which describe power as travesty, masking, card sharpers' tricks, crude peasant jokes. The failure of representation is produced by a general loss of meaning in which class interests cannot assume a form which would allow for political action based on real opposing interests. Narrative has been short-circuited.[15] In Marx's terms, the advance of revolution is deferred because the terms of class antagonism have been diffused. What is of interest here is how in Marx's account, a figure of political authority survives, through its "own" canny manipulations, the very representative function which should sustain it, and which it has both appropriated and made meaningless.

All relations of power immediately preceding and during the Second Empire are determined by internal slippages and deformations in the system of representation, exemplified for Marx by the elections of December 10, 1848 and culminating in the coup d'état in December, 1851. Once power is jarred from its legitimate bases in clearly defined lines of genealogical descent of authority, misrepresentations do, in fact, produce differing local effects during the period, which Marx discusses in detail, but it is the configuration of a generalized disruption of the system which interests me here. What are some of the complex confusions which allow the emergence of an empty subject of power, not the "son of his mother, but the nephew of his uncle," who, "because he was nothing, could signify everything but himself"?[16]

In *The 18th Brumaire*, Marx divides the period immediately preceding the election of Louis Napoléon into three parts; the February period (May 4, 1848 to May 28, 1849), the period of the constitution of the republic (May 28, 1849 to December 2, 1851) and the period of the constitutional republic. Each period is characterized by a complex disruption of sense, either in the meaning of political labels, which do not signify what they should, or, more generally, in the results of political positions assumed by various classes, which often turn out to be radically different from or even antithetical to their anticipated consequences. All of this occurs within a general movement in which the bourgeoisie ensures its dominion over the proletariat by constituting the legislature as a system of representation to serve the interests of the bourgeoisie ... only to find that government is ultimately to be handed over to the executive.

The February period, the prologue to the revolution, from the overthrow of Louis Philippe to May, 1848, and the meeting of the Constituent Assembly, was marked by a generalized loss of meaning; political reform is articulated through high-flown phrases about the general interest which conceal an irreconcilable fragmentation of its elements:

the monarchy ran away, the republic appeared to be a matter of course. Every party construed it in its own way ... In no period do we, therefore, find a more confused mixture of high-flown phrases and actual uncertainty and clumsiness, of more enthusiastic striving for innovation and more

117

thorough domination of the old routine, of more apparent harmony of the whole of society and more profound estrangement of its elements. While the Paris proletariat still revelled in the vision of the wide prospects that had opened before it and indulged in earnest discussions on social problems, the old forces of society had grouped themselves, rallied, reflected and found unexpected support in the mass of the nation, the peasants and petty bourgeois, who all at once stormed on to the political stage, after the barriers of the July monarchy had fallen.[17]

What remains constant is the power of the old forces of society, which find unexpected support in the masses of the petty bourgeoisie and the proletariat; in short, the language of reform does not represent the interests of those who made reform possible. As Marx observes later in the essay, the phrases are without content.

In the second period, that of the constituent national assembly, the founding of the bourgeois republic simply substitutes the despotism of the bourgeois republic for that of the bourgeois monarchy. In "saving" society from the proletarian class, the party of order promotes "property, family, religion, order."[18] In the process, paradoxically, it mobilizes a violence which turns upon itself: order is disorder:

Bourgeois fanatics for order are shot down on their balconies by mobs of drunken soldiers, their domestic sanctuaries profaned, their houses bombarded for amusement – in the name of property, of the family, of religion and of order.[19]

There is thus a complex disruption of the symbolic system; on the one hand, signifiers, labels and slogans are cut loose from what they presumably signify, and, on the other hand, they mask the re-emergence of the same, the oppressive state and cultural institutions.[20]

In this pervasive crisis of meaning, changed names signify nothing other than a repetition of the same:

The old organization of the administration, of the municipal system, of the judicial system, of the army, etc., continued to exist inviolate, or, where the Constitution changed it, the change concerned the table of contents; the name, not the subject matter.[21]

The royalist labels were torn off the machine of the old monarchy and republican labels were stuck on.[22]

Perhaps the most dramatic sign of the dysfunction of representation is signaled by the role of the peasants in the election of Louis Napoléon on December 10, 1848:

The symbol that expressed their entry into the revolutionary movement, clumsily cunning, knavishly naive, doltishly sublime, a calculated superstition, a pathetic burlesque, a cleverly stupid anachronism, a world historical piece of buffoonery and an undecipherable hieroglyphic for the understanding of the civilized – this symbol bore the unmistakable features of the class that represents barbarism within civilization.[23]

For the peasants, Napoléon was not a person, but a program:

With banners, with beat of drums and blare of trumpets, they marched to the polling booths shouting: "plus d'impots, à bas les riches, à bas la république, vive l'Empereur." Behind the emperor was hidden the peasant war. The republic that they voted down was the republic of the rich.[74]

Meanings attributed to this election, however, proliferate in such a way that each class attaches to it a false narrative: for the proletariat it meant the deposition of General Cavaignac and the dismissal of bourgeois republicanism; for the petty bourgeois, it meant the rule of the debtors over the creditors, the big bourgeoisie; for the bourgeoisie, Napoléon III signified the overthrow of the republic and the beginning of a royalist restoration. The ultimate irony in this play of mistaken identities is that the peasants do not constitute a class; the identity of their interests begets no community. They cannot function as a class, a social subject, for they "are" formed, homologous magnitudes as the "simple addition of so many potatoes in a sack."[25] They cannot represent themselves and, consequently, must be represented. Napoléon III, however, looks upon himself as the representative of the middle class whose interests he imposes as though it were the general interest.[26] In the name of material order, Napoléon III further weakens the peasants by adding to the tax burden and thus making them more vulnerable to the mortgage holders;[27] he sustains rule by the force of the army, itself composed not of the true peasant, but of false peasants, the "lumpenproletariat":

It [the army] consists in large measure of *remplaçants*, of substitutes, just as the second Bonaparte is himself only a *remplaçant*, the substitute for Napoléon.[28]

Finally, with the coup d'état and the triumph of executive "order," the bourgeoisie consecrates both the demise of representation and the meaninglessness of the language of general interest:

Only the chief of the Society of December 10 can still save bourgeois society! Only theft can still save property; only perjury, religion; bastardry, the family; disorder, order![29]

The scandal, for Marx, is that Napoléon III's rule represents a *caesura* in history, in which the state, which should represent the domination of one class over another, is empty of class content.[30]

119

Central to this scandal is Napoléon's relation to the middle class; "he is somebody solely due to the fact that he has broken the political power of this middle class and daily breaks it anew."[31] Napoléon, consequently, is an empty figure, which presides over a pervasive disruption of cause and effect in the general ruin of narrative and a widespread and complex crisis of meaning.

In these texts, there is a curious unresolved tension between an essentially conservative model of narrative and the radical politics promoted by the analysis. Repeated references to an implicit model of narrative based on clearly-defined oppositions between agents, and on cause and effect relationships which should produce assimilable consequences, signal a persistent motif in the essays. The sequential relations and the actantial structure of narrative agents could easily be accounted for by a greimassian analysis, which, as Jameson has noted, is grounded in ideological closure.[32] Marx does not examine the problematic underlying his rhetorical models, for it is part of the historical impasse of the times, whose resolution awaits the moment of a different order of class interests. Strategically Marx deflects the issues with explosive laughter. Unassimilable, heterogeneous elements are marked in these essays, then, by the moment of farce and by the derisive laughter it occasions. Marx's analysis is thus caught in an outmoded model of narrative, which contemporary "events" have rendered inoperative, but which he nonetheless repeats in his own text. Farce figures meanings which are unassimilable, excessive and scandalous, not to be contained by the narratives of the past, but which cannot yet be transformed into radically new narrative.[33]

The farcical, outrageous disruptions of political authority and the narratives of class interest have unexpected echoes in the official interpretations of "outrages" to public morality during the trials of Baudelaire and Flaubert in 1857. In the defense of public order these proceedings focus on signifying practices which have close affinities with those discussed by Marx and those which I have explored above in this book; again the central questions are the status of the subject and the meaning of narrative.

The documents of the trials provide an extraordinary insight into the functions of the authorial subject and narrative meaning as they are defined by law, and offer glimpses into the ways in which Flaubert's and Baudelaire's texts both repeat and radically undermine bourgeois ideology of the time. The strategies of containment brought to bear on Flaubert's novel and Baudelaire's poems in the juridical readings unerringly reveal the corrosive force exercised by these texts on the representation of power within the symbolically dominant. It is significant that the Imperial prosecutor, the voice of order, Pinard, in both trials, like Marx, must address a complex collapse of the subject and of the system of representation by which the subject interprets the "real."[34]

As Dominick La Capra has shown in his excellent "*Madame Bovary*" *on Trial*, the very restricted reading of the novel by the prosecutor and the defense is based on tacit and shared assumptions.[35] This set of conventional expectations on how things make sense and how novels are to be read focuses on the narrator and relies on a presumed equivalence between the narrator and the author, whose civic and moral being must be duplicated in recognizable ways in the literary text.[36] As La Capra has demonstrated, the defense's and prosecutor's remarks in many ways mirror each other; commenting on the same textual elements, they simply derive opposite meanings. Their analytic procedures are the same and proceed from the same notions about interpretability. Each assumes that the novel's narrative can be translated by paraphrase without loss or excess and that it is available to synoptic analysis. Nowhere do they suggest that the novel may cause concern about the validity of the criteria for interpretation, the assumptions underlying the procedures.[37]

In discussing Flaubert's trial I will select three issues common to both trial commentaries which have evident resonances with Marx's discussion of the disruptions of representation: the problem of "improper" meaning resulting from the displacement of terms from their common-sense positions; the authority of the narrator; the stable sense of the narrative signified. These problems of literary meaning are intimately related to the status of the bourgeois individual whose civil, legal and moral responsibilities should pass directly into the novel in the figure of the authoritative narrator. Each of these elements of the text and its problematic poses the question of narrative continuity and interpretability.

Pinard was troubled by a phrase which he singled out for comment; during the scene at the opera, when Emma reiterates the narrative of her "own" past in Lucie de Lammermoor's story, the narrator refers to Emma's disillusionments as "les souillures du mariage et les désillusions de l'adultère." He notes an unexpected slippage here in which the meaning anticipated is disrupted by a reversal of terms. The phrase "should" read: "les désillusions du mariage et les souillures de l'adultère." Sénard, on the other hand attempts to restore order and to elude the possible consequences of errant meanings by concentrating on the second part of the phrase in isolation. He is then able to read it quite traditionally as a "testimony to the ways in which adultery will not bring a hoped-for escape from the platitudes of marriage, but only something worse."[38] In either case, the problem has far greater significance than the potential injury inflicted on the institution of marriage by this puzzling chiasmus, for it has a profound impact on the institution of language. When one term can be substituted for another, and the closure of one paradigm opened up to the contamination of another, language is breached by transgressions of the sort that, judiciously, it is supposed to identify and contain. The referent of the questionable phrase is not unimportant, however; by singling out this particular passage, the prosecutor proves a surprising sensitivity to the interrelations between language and those institutions, like marriage, which are initiated by performative speech acts.[39] Clearly this slippage of meaning has even more wide-reaching consequences, for once the power to define and identify is undermined, the legal base of all institutions has been shaken.[40]

Both commentators place strong emphasis on the requirement that narrative be interpretable. For the defense, not surprisingly, the text is fully meaningful; it is an object lesson for the reader, depicting the dangers of adultery. As a counter-example, the narrative of Emma's transgressions invites condemnation. For the prosecutor, on the other hand, the novel doesn't provide a stable basis for interpretation, an authority for the narrative which could be assumed by a narrator or by a protagonist who represents the point of view of order:

Qui peut condamner cette femme dans le livre? Personne. Telle est la conclusion. Il n'y a pas dans le livre un personnage qui puisse la condamner. Si vous y trouvez un personnage sage, si vous y trouvez un seul principe en vertu duquel l'adultère soit stigmatisé, j'ai tort. Donc, si, dans tout le livre, il n'y a pas un personnage qui puisse lui faire courber la tête, s'il n'y a pas une idée, une ligne en vertu de laquelle l'adultère soit flétri, c'est moi qui ai raison, le livre est immoral! . . . Le condamnerez-vous au nom de la conscience de l'auteur? Je ne sais pas ce que pense la conscience de l'auteur . . .[41]

The events of the novel, furthermore, "prove" nothing. What should be a central event, the death of the protagonist, does not conform to a moral narrative; she dies because she wanted to die.[42]

For the defense, however, there is no displacement of point of view, no authorial indeterminacy; on the contrary, the intentional center of the text is said to rest not only upon the assumed equivalence between narrator and author, but on a genealogy which is firmly grounded in the law of the father. Sénard is so sure of the author's meaning that he can and does assume his voice (as La Capra noted) speaking in the first person as "Flaubert."[43] There is for Sénard, finally, a reassuring congruity between the authority of the father and that of the son (no Marxian travesties here!). Sénard sustains his defense of Flaubert's morality by linking it to the respectability of his father's position as chief surgeon at the Hôtel Dieu in Rouen.[44] Sénard thus establishes a powerful convergence between the voice of authority in literature, and those of law and science, grounded ultimately in paternity.

If Flaubert's text is indeed questionable, it is because its language threatens the order of cultural and political systems. The dominant order can survive only by denying the corrosive effects produced by decentered, dispersed subjectivity and by narrative indeterminacy, or on the other hand, by acknowledging the threat and condemning it in the very terms which the text has rendered questionable. Flaubert, then, was quite correct to recognize in dedicating *Madame Bovary* to Sénard, the "unexpected authority" which the work acquired as a result of Sénard's successful defense: "En passant par votre magnifique plaidoirie, mon oeuvre a acquis pour moi-même comme une autorité imprévue."

A brief discussion of Baudelaire's trial (August, 1857) will underscore my claim that the writing practices discussed above are part of a general and widespread disruption of the symbolic order, bearing on the expressive subject, on the proper functions of representation and on the authority which can be assumed for narrative. The imperial prosecutor, again, is Pinard and again, the question of a stable authorial voice is crucial. While Pinard judged that *Madame Bovary* was morally suspect because he was unable to establish the rhetorical/legal status of the author/narrator, the author of *Les Fleurs du mal*, in the prosecutor's view, is not only identifiable but unique. Baudelaire's voice is distinct; it is not even shared through affinities of esthetic practices with that of other authors belonging to a single "school":

Charles Baudelaire n'appartient pas à une école. Il ne relève que de lui-même.[45]

The defense concurs on this point, stating that the author is an *honnête homme*. He ascribes the success of Baudelaire's esthetic accomplishment to the worthy bourgeois value work, which, presumably, will redeem the potentially dangerous gratuitousness of art by allying it with acceptable values associated with economic productivity:

Charles Baudelaire n'est pas seulement le grand artiste et le poète profond et passionné au talent duquel l'honorable organe du ministère public a tenu lui-même à rendre un hommage public.

Il est plus: il est un honnête homme, et c'est pour cela qu'il est un artiste convaincu ... Son oeuvre, il l'a longuement meditée ... elle est le fruit de plus de huit années de travail; il l'a porté, il l'a murie dans son cerveau, avec amour, comme la femme porte dans ses entrailles l'enfant de sa tendresse.[46]

The role of a certain definition of masculine sexuality (*l'honorable organe*) is central to the legally validated system of cultural representations, and any disequilibrium introduced by deviance from the norm must be addressed as a threat. Here, in comparing Baudelaire's responsibility as the masculine author, who conceives his text in meditation, with that of a mother for the child she nurtures and bears, and in thus linking two metaphors of artistic generation, the defense, as I will later show, produces resonances whose importance or effects he could hardly have anticipated. For the moment, however, I simply wish to note that the first concern of a legal reading of the texts is to establish the integrity of the author/narrator as a full, expressive subject. The author/narrator must be accountable to a system of order sustained by a metaphorics of male dominance.

Although the moral grounds of the accusations are both religious and sexual, they share a common element; they establish a space within which law and religion must contain transgression: "la seule base solide de nos moeurs publiques."[47]

Pinard's pronouncement about the judge as an interpreter of literature echoes "Les Phares" in an uncanny parody:

Le juge n'est point un critique littéraire ... le législateur ... a donné au pouvoir judiciaire une autorité discretionnaire pour reconnaître si cette morale est offensée, si la limite a été franchie. Le juge est une sentinelle qui ne doit pas laisser passer la frontière. Voilà sa mission.[48]

The "sentinel effect," noted above in my discussion of Baudelaire's allegories, which opens the text to the echoes of a virtually limitless reverberation of meaning, is here marshalled to maintain closure within the boundaries of accepted social practice. This is a system of representation which depends on "recognition" of what is acceptable and what is different and therefore deviant. Baudelaire's excesses, the celebrated bizarreries of style are outlandish, then, in more than esthetic terms.[49]

In acknowledging the seductiveness of Baudelaire's art, the prosecutor professes a certain uneasiness about how the texts will be read, noting that no reader is entirely "healthy," since all are more or less vulnerable to the "poisons" of the imagination. He suggests indirectly that the threat to divide and fragment the subject, the reader in this instance, is a powerful attack on a moral order whose "solid base" is the subject itself. The entire structure of the author/reader dyad, the *je/tu* of expressive communication, is threatened. Although Pinard does not explore the implications of the questions raised by his discussion of the reader's vulnerabilities, we can assume that the anxious attention he devotes to this problem proceeds from an intuitive understanding that, as Benveniste has shown, the positions of *je* and *tu* are reversible; the integrity or fragmentation of one element of the dyad, presupposes that of the other.[50] The two trials read together, then, pronounce the death of the subject, long before Mallarmé's "Crise de vers":

Même vos lecteurs instruits, chez vos hommes faits, croyez-vous qu'il y ait beaucoup de froids calculateurs pesant le pour et le contre, mettant le contre-poids à côté du poids, ayant la tête, l'imagination, les sens parfaitement équilibrés? L'homme n'en veut pas convenir, il a trop d'orgueil pour cela. Mais la vérité, la voici. l'homme est toujours plus ou moins infirme, plus ou moins faible, plus ou moins malade, portant d'autant plus le poids de sa chute originelle, qu'il veut en douter ou la nier. Si telle est sa nature intime tant qu'elle n'est pas relevée par de mâles efforts et une forte discipline, qui ne sait combien il prendra facilement le goût des frivolités lascives, sans se préoccuper de l'enseignement que l'auteur veut y placer.[51]

Things would be better, according to the prosecutor, if the book were not distributed so widely, so inexpensive that it is likely to fall into the hands of "ces lecteurs multiples, de tout rang, de tout âge, de toute condition . . ."[52] The problem suggests the collision of two radically different economies of dissemination, the first securely closed within a paternal authority, the second uncontrollably open, promiscuously available.[53] But even in opposing the multiple readers, with their shaky economic and cultural condition, to the *homme fait*, secure in his cultural capital, the prosecutor is forced to admit that every reader is vulnerable, because he is divided from within.

The integrity of even the ideal reader subject, paradoxically is menaced by an unassimilable excess:

De bonne foi, croyez-vous qu'on puisse tout dire, tout peindre, tout mettre à nu ... Ou le sens de la pudeur n'existe pas, ou la limite qu'elle impose a été audacieusement franchise.[54]

The *tout*, the excess which must be censored, we will see in reading some of the texts finally condemned, and passages quoted in the prosecutor's speech, is threatening because it cannot be contained within the space of male cultural discipline. The term *tout* is advanced as a stereotype designating a finite set of meanings, which would be unveiled ultimately as the final, hidden truth (*mettre à nu*); however, the term *tout* functions here more like the signifier of unassimilable excess, in a system of infinitely deferred meaning.

Tout is divided from within and menaced by unstable relations of difference, evidenced most dramatically in the texts by the figuration of erotic objects. While it is not surprising to find that female sexuality is the principal carrier of unhealthy disorder (figured with anxious disgust as a phobic object in "Les Métamorphoses du vampire" as "une outre aux flancs gluants, toute pleine de pus!"), there is a radical and diverse disjunction of the "polarities" of heterosexual order at work here. In "Lesbos," and "Les Femmes damnées," sapphic eroticism problematizes the active/passive hierarchy based on the model of the heterosexual couple. More importantly, difference is internalized and unrecognizable to a male viewing subject. "Deviant" sexuality, by ignoring the "fact" of castration, constitutes a powerful threat to a legal system, which is overseen, as I noted above, by the "honorable organ" of the public ministry.

The locus of erotic activity is obscenely displaced in "A Celle qui est trop gaie," which is perhaps more offensive for the doubling and decentering of the erotic object than for its sadistic theme:

> Ainsi je voudrais, une nuit
> Quand l'heure des voluptés sonne
> Sur les trésors de ta personne,
> Comme un lâche, ramper sans bruit,
>
> Pour châtier ta chair joyeuse,
> Pour meurtrir ton sein pardonné,
> Et faire à ton flanc étonné
> Une blessure large et creuse,

Et vertigineuse douceur!
A travers ces lèvres nouvelles,
Plus éclatantes et plus belles,
T'infuser mon venin, ma soeur!

In "Les Bijoux," the familiar abundant, voluptuous contours of a female body are supplemented by the ambivalent sexuality of a male adolescent:

Je croyais voir unis par un nouveau dessin
Les hanches de l'Antiope au buste d'un imberbe,
Tant sa taille faisait ressortir son bassin.
Sur ce teint fauve et brun, le fard était superbe!

The crucial issues for the prosecutor, then, concern a disruption of an expressive model of communication and a concurrent threat to the ideal order of desire, an order which is ultimately grounded in the legal status of the subject. Baudelaire as author of his texts is unique and responsible, but he must be taken to account because he produces divisions within the ideal reader, fragmenting a subject which can only be contained by a virile discipline of patriarchal order. The balance of the specular schema is destroyed when one element of the dyad becomes unrecognizable, and that reflects on the speaking subject, of course, and the system of order which he bodies forth. Once difference has been introduced into this model, the only solution is to recognize that otherness by setting it outside the boundaries of social discourse. The second area of concern is the erotic body, with its errant and fragmented objects of desire, which introduces unresolvable instabilities within the definitions of sexual identity. Difference which can be contained within the boundaries of heterosexuality, even though it may produce phobic revulsion, as in "Les Métamorphoses du vampire," is a lesser threat to social order than lesbianism, which the prosecutor refers to with technical, though unnecessarily limiting precision, as tribadism, or, as in the example from "Les Bijoux," the mixing of sexual "properties," in the ambiguous combination of female thighs with a male adolescent bust. Sexuality is figured here as an ungraspable *between*, which problematizes the hierarchical dyad on which acceptable representations of the erotic are founded. Like the "new lips" in "A Celle qui est trop gaie," deviance is a wound to an integral body of representations, and constitutes a significant menace to a wider system of patriarchal authority. In short, the integrity of the erotic body is intimately linked to a system of relations which sustain the body politic.

127

Returning briefly to the passage quoted from the opening statement of the speech by the defense, we can draw out the broader meanings of Chaix d'Este Ange's mixed metaphors of generation. By combining the conceptual activity of a paternal *honnête homme* with the figure of the nurturing mother, this conceit produces complex, though only obliquely acknowledged, disturbances of the sexual metaphorics of power. Taken separately, each of these metaphors of generation could pass unnoticed as a cliché, but in this context the passage undermines those very universalized values which both prosecution and defense seek to uphold. The mixed metaphor is a sign of a more radical mix-up than might be expected, and threatens structures far more widespread than those of the conventional esthetic order.[55] The initial sexual confusion may be read as a subtext to what follows in my discussion of the defense's efforts to keep things straight.

Chaix d'Este Ange attempts to contain a contradiction in his own discourse; that between the claim that there is a univocal meaning to the poems and the acknowledgment that one may in fact be led astray, seduced, by a few random, expressive details which are exaggerated and violent. His initial reading, however, eliminates detail by subjecting the texts to paraphrase; his second reading returns to a residue as yet unaccounted for, those very details which were initially said to be non-essential.

To prove the moral responsibility of the author and the univocal status of meaning, Chaix d'Este Ange first invites the judge to cast off the "superficial form" of the texts, in order to retrieve the "sincere intention" of the author:

ce n'est pas la forme qu'il faut interroger, mais le fond; et l'on risquerait fort de se tromper et de ne pas faire bonne et équitable justice, si l'on se laissait entrainer par quelques expressions, exagerées et violentes, parsemées çà et là, sans aller au fond des choses, sans rechercher les intentions sincères, sans se rendre un compte bien exact de l'esprit qui anime le livre.[56]

As in the legal commentaries of *Madame Bovary*, the defense assumes that the text can be paraphrased without any loss of significance, yet there is an added element of particular importance here: the language of truth is the language of prose. Having quoted several stanzas of "Au Lecteur," the peroration to the hypocritical reader, the defense states:

Transformez cela en prose, messieurs, supprimez la rime et la césure, recherchez ce qu'il y a au fond de ce langage puissant et imagé, quelles intentions s'y cachent; et dites-moi si nous n'avons jamais entendu tomber ce même langage du haut de la chaire chrétienne, et des lèvres de quelque prédicateur ardent; dites-moi si nous ne trouverions pas les mêmes pensées, et quelquefois peut-être les mêmes expressions dans les homélies de quelque rude et sévère père de l'Eglise?[57]

It is quite acceptable to appropriate the voice of the text if, unlike the unspeakable image of "A Celle qui est trop gaie," it remains within the figuration of authority and truth. According to the defense, Baudelaire's text speaks the elevated language of the moralist; he thus identifies truth and the power it represents with prose. If pushed to its ultimate consequences, the defense's argument would be forced to admit that poetry is culpable from the start, for it can become truthful only when its generic markers, rhyme and rhythm, have been "suppressed," that is, when it becomes prose. Baudelaire's "method," according to this reading is consistent with classical rhetorical definitions of poetry as an ornament of discourse; the ultimate meaning would depend not on the ornamental, superfluous form, but on a kernel, prose sense.[58] The defense, furthermore, cannot dispense with the troublesome details, which appear in his argument as an unassimilable excess in the system of representation. The claim is that, in showing vice in all its detail, Baudelaire intends to render it odious.[59] The stakes are high, and the metaphor chosen by the defense indicates that what is at issue here is the integrity of a complex and far-reaching system of representation: "sous peine de prendre la fausse monnaie à l'égal de la bonne, il faut distinguer entre l'hypocrisie et la dévotion; ..."[60] The passage refers to Tartuffe (surely a particularly dissonant irony for Baudelaire, whose truculent evaluations of Molière suggest how inappropriate the allusion may have been), but there is more to the example than the analogy with another great work which was misunderstood in its time. Because Baudelaire's "painting" of vice is to be taken as a counter-example, not as hypocritically seductive, his "own" language can be considered hard currency. In reading the poems of revolt, he inverts the role of the hypocrite by having the poet assume the voice of blasphemy for ultimately moral ends. The blasphemies are not uttered in "his own" voice, nor are the intentions expressed by the voice of the text "his own": "les sentiments qu'il exprime ne sont pas les siens."[61] On the other hand, it is possible for the defense to distinguish the poet's own thoughts and language, "son propre langage," "ses propres pensées," in the hymn of "Les Phares" ("Soyez béni mon Dieu, qui donnez la souffrance ...")'.[62] The unique, true voice of the poet, *le propre*, is thus intimately bound, as the initial metaphor indicates, to a wider symbolic system of representation, which includes not only moral order but the political and economic. The proper is based on the gold standard.[63]

The monetary metaphor is summoned here to redeem Baudelaire's language from a double contradiction, which indicates once again how much is at issue when it comes to considerations of generic boundaries and their stability. Baudelaire's poetry ultimately "is" prose, because its real kernel has been regained through prose paraphrase; both narrative and authorial subject thus remain intact. The excessive detail, however, cannot be dismissed and the real prose ... turns out to be still poetry. Thus the defense's speech, in seeking to establish the rightful consistency of Baudelaire's texts, produces instead an intricate web of discontinuities, which are intimately associated with a generalized breakdown of a system of representation and the prose discourse which subtends it.[64]

The final sequence in Chaix d'Este Ange's blind deconstructive reading attempts to bring *Les Fleurs du mal* back on to safe ground by showing that their excesses are in no way eccentric, that outrageous details may be found in the writings of celebrated contemporaries, such as Lamartine, Musset, Béranger and Gautier. The strategy, of course, is innocence by association, to be established by inserting Baudelaire's poems into a culturally acceptable intertext. The quotations are examples of the almost outrageous; they go to the limits of respectability, but if they are to serve their purpose in the defense's reading, they could hardly be expected to pass the sentinel's frontier. What is it which justifies their place among culturally acceptable representations? In attempting to answer that questiion, I will show that they only further confirm the threat posed to those representations by *Les Fleurs du mal*; like the mixed metaphors of the authorial generation, these examples produce deviant progeny.

Although he undercuts another argument crucial to this defense, that *Les Fleurs du mal* must be read as a whole, sustained by the secret architecture of the book and not judged on fragments disjoined from their context, Chaix d'Este Ange excerpts several texts without regard for their context.[65] The passages are cited as examples of revolt against religion, or as titillating erotic representations. The examples given, however, are no threat to the cultural symbolic order which the court oversees precisely because the meaning of their context is so unambiguous. The integrity of the expressive subject is never questioned, and it speaks within the clear confines of an assimilable narrative. In fact, the passages quoted demonstrate by counter-example the deeply disturbing impact of Baudelaire's poems.[66]

The passages purported to be sexually titillating all remain securely within the space of accepted transgressions which can be tolerated by bourgeois heterosexuality, that "difference" charged with reaffirming the primacy of the self-same. The eulogy of nudity in Musset's poem describes nudity as the unadorned, "heroic" essence of humanity;

> Tout est nu sur la terre, hormis l'hypocrisie;
> Tout est nu dans les cieux, tout est nu dans la vie,
> Les tombeaux, les enfants et les divinités,
> Tous les coeurs vraiment beaux laissent voir leurs beautés.
> Ainsi donc le héros de cette comédie,
> Restera nu, madame, – et vous y consentez.[67]

In a passage from Béranger, a grandmother's account of her pre-marital sexual exploits and those after the death of her husband takes its place in a hereditary line of transgression which is, precisely, an accepted deviation from the model of conjugal sex. The glib allusion here to celebrations of the "saint" in the temple of love, though it serves as a figure for female sexual anatomy, simply underscores the survival of phallic supremacy in the old woman's not so errant desire. The poem is a dialog between a little girl and her grandmother:

> Bien tard, maman, vous fûtes veuve?
> – Oui, mais grâce à ma gaité,
> Si l'église n'était pas neuve
> Le saint n'en fut pas moins fêté.
>
> Comme vous, maman, faut-il faire?
> – Et! mes petits-enfants, pourquoi,
> Quand j'ai fait comme ma grand'mère,
> Ne feriez-vous pas comme moi?[68]

The final excerpt from Gautier's *Mademoiselle de Maupin*, introduces a certain eccentric element into my argument, since it is taken from a story of transvestism, but that misrepresentation is redeemed in the passage quoted, in which the body of the heroine, Rosalinde, is unveiled at the moment she is to enter into "true" femininity, when she yields to her lover. She confesses that she is a virgin and D'Albert, her companion, begins a symbolic *dépucellage* by removing her clothes, setting "free" her sexual identity:

131

D'Albert, singulièrement ému, lui prit les mains et en baisa tous les doigts, les uns après les autres, puis rompit fort délicatement le lacet de la robe, en sorte que le corsage s'ouvrit et que les deux blancs trésors apparurent dans toute leur splendeur.

The sexual enigma is now transparent:

Elle demeura tout debout comme une blanche apparition avec une simple chemise de la toile la plus transparente. La chemise douée d'un heureux esprit d'imitation ne resta pas en arriere de la robe . . .[69]

Finally, she is the figure of mimetic representation, a woman/ statue, the "perfect resemblance" of the model of the real:

– Ainsi posée, elle ressemblait parfaitement à ces statues de marbre des déesses, dont la draperie intelligente, fachée de recouvrir tant de charmes, enveloppe à regret les belles cuisses, et, par une heureuse trahison, s'arrète precisément au-dessous de l'endroit qu'elle est destinée à cacher. – Mais, comme la chemise n'était pas de marbre et que ses plis ne la soutenaient pas, elle continua sa triomphale descente . . .[70]

This elegant striptease simply reinforces the assumptions under-lying the defense's speech, and which Baudelaire's poems repeatedly question; when the truth is unveiled, its contours are recognizable and available to appropriation by a male subject, whose essence and desires, sustained by the law, are reflected back to him, undistorted by difference. According to this view of things, the subject is indeed there where he would be; the objects of his desire located in a secure hierarchy between masculine and femin-ine in a narrative untroubled by deviance from a familiar *telos*.

I would like to end by reflecting on the problem of questions and answers, as it relates to the structural similarities in the figuration of the subject, the design of narrative and the status of the narrative signified in those literary, historical and juridical texts that I have read in this final chapter. Unable to ask the question of its question the symbolic operations of a changing political system, analyzed by Marx in his discussion of the configurations of power in the second Napoleonic period, and those summoned up in the speeches of the court of the Imperial prosecutor, attempt to advance a set of answers about power and meaning in order to sustain an always questionable discourse of authority. When pressed by analysis in the terms provided by our study of fiction, the dominant discourse begins to undo and dismantle itself, revealing its fissures where it meets those troublesome questions posed by the literary texts. The internal coherence of the system of the culturally dominant relies on certain symbolic processes, which are bodied forth in order to support the subject of authority and its own narrative of power. This is a complex system of misrepresentations that the literary texts I have discussed repeatedly question by asking the questions that the agents of political order could pose only at the expense of their own dominance. The insistent, corrosive force of the literary text is, in large measure, this very power to engage the problematic of the social discourse by interrogating its silent question. The literary question is of a different order, as I noted in my introduction, quoting Barthes; it is never a direct "pure question," but a complex of traces, disseminated throughout the text: "... dispersée en fragments entre lesquelles le sens fuse et fuit tout à la fois."

NOTES

Introduction

1 Michel Foucault, *Les Mots et les Choses* (Paris: Gallimard, "Bibliothèque des sciences humaines," 1966), 397.

2 Stéphane Mallarmé, "Crise de vers," *Oeuvres complètes*, ed. Henri Mondor, G. Jean-Aubry (Paris: Gallimard, "Bibliothèque de la Pléiade," 1945), 366. All references to Mallarmé are to this edition.

3 Foucault in *Les Mots et les Choses*, has shown that nineteenth-century, post-classical thought can no longer think of being and thought as consubstantial: "Dans le cogito moderne, il s'agît ... de laisser valoir selon sa plus grande dimension la distance qui à la fois sépare et relie la pensée présente à soi, et ce qui, de la pensée, s'enracine dans le non pensé; il lui faut ... parcourir, redoubler et réactiver sous une forme explicite l'articulation de la pensée sur ce qui en elle, autour d'elle, au-dessous d'elle n'est pas pensée, mais ne lui est pas pour autant étranger, selon une irréductible, une infranchissable extériorité," 335. There is a crucial slippage from the mode of assertion to that of hypothesis:
> "que faut-il que je sois, moi qui pense et qui suis ma pensée, pour que je sois ce que je ne pense pas, pour que ma pensée soit ce que je ne suis pas?" 335–6.

4 "Orage, lustral; et, dans des bouleversements, tout à l'acquit de la genération, récente, l'acte d'écrire se scruta jusqu'en l'origine. Très avant, au moins, quant au point, je le formule: – A savoir s'il y a lieu d'écrire." "La Musique et les lettres," 645.

5 Roland Barthes, "Littérature et Signification," *Essais critiques* (Paris: Seuil, 1964), 261.

1. The Danaides Vessel: on reading Baudelaire's allegories

1 See my "Stylistic Functions of Rhetoric in Baudelaire's 'Au Lecteur,'" *Kentucky Romance Quarterly*, vol. 19, no. 4 (1972), 447–60. In his recent study of Walter Benjamin, Terry Eagleton discusses the latent connection between symbolism's denigration of allegory in favor of the symbol and the valorization of speech over writing: "Symbolism has denigrated allegory as thoroughly as the ideology of the speaking voice

134

has humiliated script; and though Benjamin himself does not fully develop the connection, it is surely a relevant one. For the allegorical object has undergone a kind of haemorrhage of spirit: drained of all immanent meaning, it lies as a pure facticity under the manipulative hand of the allegorist, awaiting such meaning as he or she may imbue it with. Nothing could more aptly exemplify such a condition than the practice of writing itself, which draws its atomized material fragments into endless, unmotivated constellations of meaning." *Walter Benjamin, Or Towards a Revolutionary Criticism* (London and New York: Verso Editions and Schocken Books, 1981), 6. These remarks have a special pertinence to our study of Baudelaire's verse, for, as Benjamin notes in his essay "On Some Motifs in Baudelaire," *Illuminations*, transl. Harry Zohn (New York: Schocken Books, 1969), 155–200, the poems of *Les Fleurs du mal* have an uneasy relation with the enabling fiction of the lyric, the presumed continuity between experience and a lyric "voice."

2 Charles Baudelaire, "Le Poème du haschish" in *Oeuvres complètes*, ed. Y.-G. Le Dantec, Claude Pichois (Paris: Gallimard, "Bibliothèque de la Pléiade, " 1961), 376. All quotations from Baudelaire are taken from this edition.

3 For a discussion of this opposition between allegorical and symbolic modes that merged in the literature of England, Germany and France in the late-eighteenth century and early-nineteenth century, see: Meyer Abrams, "Structure and Style in the Greater Romantic Lyric" in *From Sensibility to Romanticism: Essays Presented to F. A. Pottle*, ed. F. W. Hillis and H. Bloom (New York: Oxford University Press, 1965); Paul de Man, "The Rhetoric of Temporality," in *Interpretation: Theory and Practice*, ed. C. S. Singleton (Baltimore: Johns Hopkins University Press, 1969), 285; H.-G. Gadamer, *Truth and Method*, transl. and ed. by G. Barden and J. Cumming (New York: Seabury Press, 1975); T. Todorov, *Théories du symbole* (Paris: Seuil, 1977); W. K. Wimsatt, "The Structure of Romantic Nature Imagery" in *The Verbal Icon* (Lexington, KY: University of Kentucky Press, 1967).

4 de Man, "The Rhetoric of Temporality," 174; Gadamer, *Truth and Method*, 63–73.

5 Baudelaire, "L'Art philosophique," 1101. Baudelaire groups different semiotic processes in the four terms *allégorie, allusion, hiéroglyphe, rébus*, what is of interest to me here is the common link provided by the term *translation*, which supposes a separation between levels of meaning and a correlation to be established rationally between them.

6 See de Man, "The Rhetoric of Temporality," on Coleridge, 177–9; Todorov, "Symbole et allégorie" in *Théories du symbole*, on Goethe and Schelling, 235–59.

7 See J. Derrida, *Positions* (Paris: Minuit, 1972), 57–64, for a summary of distinctions between meaning considered as accessible to thematic (polysemic) readings and meaning as *dissémination*, a non-finite

number of semantic effects. See also "La Double Séance" in *La Dissémination* (Paris: Seuil, 1972).
8 de Man, "The Rhetoric of Temporality," 190.
9 The expression appears in the opening pages of "Du Vin et du hachish," 323, in which Baudelaire criticizes Brillat-Savarin's *Physiologie du Goût* for its blindness to the poetic properties of wine: "Vous aurez beau feuilleter le volume, le retourner dans tous les sens, le lire à rebours, à l'envers, de droite à gauche et de gauche à droite, ... " The passage is an invitation to disrupt the traditionally linear, metonymic process of reading and anticipates better-known statements by Mallarmé and Rimbaud.
10 See Freud's discussion of involuntary repetition as the return of material repressed by consciousness: "The Uncanny," in *On Creativity and the Unconscious*, ed. B. Nelson (New York: Harper and Row, 1958), 122–61; *Beyond the Pleasure Principle*, ed. J. Strachey (New York: Norton, 1961). On the relationship between literature and madness, see Shoshana Felman, *La Folie et la Chose littéraire* (Paris: Seuil, 1978), and on narratives of madness, Ross Chambers, "Récits d'aliénés, récits aliénés," *Poétique*, 53 (Février, 1983), 72–90.

2. On certain relations: figures of sexuality in Baudelaire

1 Page references are to Charles Baudelaire, *Oeuvres complètes*, ed. Y.-G. Le Dantec, Claude Pichois (Paris: Gallimard, "Pléiade," 1961).
2 Barbara Johnson, *Défigurations du langage poétique* (Paris: Flammarion, 1979), 13–29.
3 For discussions of Freud's texts on femininity and the construction of male "identity" in hierarchical figurations of sexuality, see Luce Irigaray, *Speculum de l'autre femme* (Paris: Minuit, 1974) particularly the chapters "La Tache aveugle d'un vieux rêve de symétrie," 162, and "Toute Théorie de sujet," 165–82. See also Sara Kofman, *L'Enigme de la femme: La femme dans les textes de Freud* (Paris: Galilée, 1980). See the final chapter of this book "The trials of authority under Louis Bonaparte," for a discussion of the ideological and legal implications of this construction of the male subject.
4 Leo Bersani, *Baudelaire and Freud* (Berkeley and Los Angeles: University of California Press, "Quantum Books," 1977). The discussion which follows draws upon my review article of Bersani's book: "Effects and Affects of Theory: Reading Bersani on Baudelaire and Freud," *Diacritics*, 9, No. 4 (Winter, 1979), 13–27.
5 Bersani, 15.
6 Bersani, 12.
7 Bersani, 13.
8 *Défigurations*: "Ce qui est visé, dans cette première phrase de la *Dédicace* comme dans la dernière, c'est la hiérarchie, la suprématie de la *tête*. La maîtrise de la volonté créatrice, comme l'identité de la chose

faite, sont éclatées par une *différence* qui remplace la puissance du travail toujours ailleurs ... Ce qui vient en tête de l'ouvrage, c'est l'absence de tête; oeuvre décapitée, mais qui se situe précisément dans la 'capitale ... ,' " 27–8.

9 Bersani, 126.

10 Virginia Swain, "The Legitimation Crisis: Event and Meaning in Baudelaire's 'Le Vieux Saltimbanque,' and 'Une Mort héroique,' " *Romanic Review*, 73, No. 4 (Nov., 1982), 452–62, discusses the erosion of the narrator's authority and the role of this conclusion in maintaining the illusion of the power.

11 On the importance of feminine sublimation in maintaining the primacy of the Phallus in Freud's account of feminine desire, see Irigaray, *Speculum*, 125–6.

12 See Kofman, *L'Enigme* ... , 260.

13 *Défigurations*: "le thyrse est une figure du rapport entre le littéral et le figuré, mais de sorte que l'expression même de ce rapport, étant elle-même une figure qui se réfère indéfiniment à d'autres figures, fait éclater la possibilité d'isoler et de distinguer entre le figuré et le littéral, entre le 'poétique' et le prosaique, pour donner un sens 'propre' à leurs rapports," 65.

14 Walter Benjamin, "On Some Motifs in Baudelaire," *Illuminations*, transl. Harry Zohn (New York: Schocken Books, 1969), 155–200. Benjamin's interesting discussion of this passage points to the importance of the crowd in Baudelaire's writings as an amorphous mass which does not stand for a collective. The crowd is a hidden configuration: "the meaning of the hidden configuration ... probably is this: it is the phantom crowd of the words, the fragments, the beginnings of lines from which the poet, in the deserted streets, wrests the poetic booty," 165.

15 Following Jacques Derrida's analysis of the strategy of the framing; "La Parergon," *Digraphe*, II (Paris: Galilée, 1974), 21–57, Sima Godfrey suggests that the pane of glass in "Les Fenêtres" functions in a manner analogous to the supplementary frame. The glass, like the frame, defines the work of art and responds to a fundamental loss or absence that is presupposed "within" the work. Baudelaire draws our attention to these frames become text; he "challenges us, the reader-spectator to look beyond the center of the poems for the implied borders that invest our reading with order." Sima Godfrey, "Baudelaire's Windows," *L'Esprit créateur*, 22, No. 4 (Winter, 1982), 83–100, esp. 91.

16 For a discussion of a self-conscious, ironic cultivation of artifice in sensuality, in Baudelaire's early novella "La Fanfarlo," see my "The Poetics of Irony in Baudelaire's 'La Fanfarlo.' " *Neophilologus*, LIX, No. 2 (April, 1985), 165–89.

17 Philippe Hamon, *Introduction à l'analyse de descriptif* (Paris: Hachette, 1981) discusses the "pleasure of description," which derives

from the generative power of language. Description, Hamon suggests, "serait peut-être cet endroit du texte où la puissance générative du langage se montrerait sous son aspect le plus évident et le plus incontrôlable," 30.

3. Emma's stories: narrative, repetition and desire in *Madame Bovary*

1 All references to *Madame Bovary* are to the Garnier edition (Paris: Garnier, 1961). References to Flaubert's other writings are to the *Oeuvres complètes* (Paris: Seuil, "L'Intégrale," 1964).

2 Of the many studies which treat the problematic of language and writing in Flaubert, and in particular in *Madame Bovary*, I have found the following to be most valuable: Charles Bernheimer, *Flaubert and Kafka: Studies in Psychopoetic Structure* (New Haven and London: Yale University Press, 1982); Leo Bersani, *A Future for Astyanax* (Boston-Toronto: Little, Brown, 1976), 89–105; Victor Brombert, *The Novels of Flaubert* (Princeton: Princeton University Press, 1966); Dominick La Capra, *Madame Bovary on Trial* (Ithaca and London: Cornell University Press, 1982); Jonathan Culler, *Flaubert: The Uses of Uncertainty* (Ithaca, NY: Cornell University Press, 1974); Alain de Lattre, *La Bêtise d'Emma Bovary* (Paris: Corti, 1980); Françoise Gaillard, "L'En-signement du réel," in *La Production du sens chez Flaubert*, ed. C. Gothot-Mersch, Colloque de Cérisy (Paris: Union générale d'éditions, 10/18, 1975), 197–220; "La Représentation comme mis en scène du voyeurisme," *RSH* vol. 154, no. 2 (1874), 267–82; Jean Rousset, *Forme et signification* (Paris: Corti, 1962), 109–33; Jean-Paul Sartre, *L' Idiot de la famille*, II (Paris: Gallimard, 1971), 1611–20; III (Paris: Gallimard, 1972), 178–201; Naomi Schor, "Pour une thématique restreinte: Ecriture, parole et différence dans *Madame Bovary*," *Litt.* 22 (1975), 30–46; R. J. Sherrington, *Three Novels by Flaubert* (Oxford: Clarendon Press, 1970); Tony Tanner, *Adultery in the Novel* (Baltimore and London: The Johns Hopkins Press, 1979), 233–367; Albert Thibaudet, *Gustave Flaubert* (Paris: Gallimard, 1935); Anthony Thorlby, *Gustave Flaubert and the Art of Realism* (London: Bowes and Bowes, 1956). Most of these analyses, in so far as they offer any extended study of Emma's stories, treat them as framed by the narrative of an authoritative narrator. Although that perspective must be taken into account, this chapter will focus more directly on Emma's stories and will trace their effects on a general interpretation of narrative in the novel. Reversing the conventional perspective produces unanticipated effects which lead to a re-examination of framing, desire and the impulses of power in narrative.

3 Roland Barthes, *S/Z* (Paris: Seuil, 1970), 146: "Flaubert ..., en maniant une ironie frappée d'incertitude, opère un malaise salutaire de l'écriture: il n'arrête pas le jeu des codes (ou l'arrête mal), en sorte que (c'est là sans doute la *preuve* de l'écriture) *on ne sait jamais s'il est*

responsable de ce qu'il écrit (s'il y a un sujet *derrière* son langage); car l'être de l'écriture (le sens du travail qui la constitue) est d'empêcher de jamais répondre à cette question: *Qui parle?*"

4 For a discussion of the combination of impersonal narration and *erlebte Rede*, or free, indirect discourse in *Madame Bovary* see Hans Robert Jauss, "Literary History as a Challenge to Literary Theory," *New Literary History*, II, No. 1 (1970), 7–38.

5 Culler, 109–22.

6 The troublesome word "reality" will assert itself frequently in my text. I will define my uses of the term here to avoid the repeated intrusion of cumbersome definitions in the course of my discussion. On the one hand, the term will refer to what the fiction designates as real, what is generally understood as an *effet de réel*. See Roland Barthes, "L'Effet de réel," *Communications*, 11 (1968), 84–9. In other instances the meaning of the term will be closer to what Lacan has called *le Réel*, which, precisely, cannot be named and resists symbolization. The *Real* can only be approximated by narrative in asymptotic fashion, as Frederic Jameson has noted: "Imaginary and Symbolic in Lacan: Marxism, Psychoanalytic Criticism and the Problem of the Subject," *Yale French Studies*, 55/56 (1977), 338–95, esp. 383–95. Very often in reading *Madame Bovary* it is not possible to assert with any confidence which of these two senses is appropriate and much of the force of the novel is generated by this indeterminacy.

7 Gaillard, "L'En-signement du réel": "on ne peut triompher de l'écriture qu'en s'absorbant en elle: par un mouvement vertigineux de répétition en abîme, il faut être le livre en recopiant le livre que l'on recopie dans le livre," 201.

8 Naomi Schor's very suggestive article, "Pour une Thématique restreinte," discusses the similarities between Homais and Emma, both of whom aspire to be writers. It should also be noted that, as interpreters, Emma and Homais are set in opposition to each other at the end of the novel. On the legal implications of a stable narrative signified see La Capra, *Madame Bovary on Trial* and the final chapter of this book.

9 Luce Irigaray, in *Speculum de l'autre femme* (Paris: Minuit, 1974), 9–162, discusses the displacement of a feminine libidinal economy and the imposition of masculine mimetic models of desire in the Freudian theory of sexual difference. In Freud's analysis of the early relation between the daughter and her mother, the young girl's role is determined by that of the male child; the daughter is said to understand her sexual difference as a lack, a defect, an absence of the phallus. The terms in which Irigaray discusses this suppression of feminine difference and its assimilation by the story of masculine desire are strikingly pertinent to this crucial passage in *Madame Bovary* : "Laissée au *vide*, au *manque* de toute représentation, re-presentation, et en toute rigueur aussi mimésis, de son désire (d')origine. Lequel en passera, dès lors,

par le désir-discours-loi du désir de l'homme: tu seras ma femme-mère, ma femme si tu veux, tu peux, être (comme) ma mère = tu seras pour moi la possibilité de répéter-représenter-reproduire-m'approprier le (mon) rapport à l'origine … Mais disons qu'*au commencement s'arrêterait son histoire*, [l'histoire de la fillette] pour se laisser prescrire par celle d'un autre: celle de l'homme père," 47.

10 See de Lattre's discussion of the "paradox of the image," *La Bêtise . . .* , 20.

11 Laurent Jenny, "Il n'y a pas de récit cathartique," *Poétique*, 41 (février, 1980), 1–21. "Cette douleur impossible, c'est celle, pour un sujet, de ne pouvoir se conjuguer au noyau verbal de son fantasme, dans la syntaxe d'une narration," 7.

12 Paradoxically, Emma seeks a fully expressive, unmediated language of desire by imitating, as if they were "her own," the stories of others' passion. In the most fundamental way, the possibility of appropriating meaning for the self is determined as a process of censorship imposed by discourse. The language of "self-expression" imposes what Pierre Bourdieu has called *euphémisation*: "toute expression est un ajustement entre un *intérêt expressif* et une *censure* constituée par la structure du champ dans lequel s'offre cette expression, et cet ajustement est le produit d'un travail d'euphémisation pouvant aller jusqu'au silence, limite du discours censuré." "La Censure," in *Questions de sociologie* (Paris: Minuit, 1980), 138.

13 Gérard Genette, *Figures* III (Paris: Seuil, 1972), 90.

14 Genette, "Silences de Flaubert," *Figures* (Paris: Seuil, 1966), 223–43.

15 On illocutionary speech acts, see Mary Louise Pratt, *Toward a Speech Act Theory of Literary Discourse* (Bloomington, London: Indiana University Press, 1977), 80–1.

16 de Lattre, *La Bêtise . . .* , 20–1.

17 C. Clément, H. Cixous, *La Jeune née* (Paris: Union générale d'éditions, 10/18, 1975), 144–7: Irigaray, *Speculum*, 165–82.

18 The term *denial* is used in Freud's sense; the subject formulates a repressed desire or thought, while denying that desire (*Verneinung*, translated in French as *dénégation*).

19 Tanner, *Adultery in the Novel*, 292–6.

20 The phatic function in language establishes, prolongs or discontinues communication. In Jakobson's terms, it is the "set for contact." R. Jakobson, "Linguistics and Poetics," in *Style in Language*, ed. Thos. Sebeok (Cambridge, Mass.: M.I.T. Press, 1960), 350–77.

21 S. Felman, "Gustave Flaubert: Folie et cliché," in *La Folie et la chose littéraire* (Paris: Seuil, 1978), 159–213; Gaillard, "L'En-signement," 198–9.

22 On narrators' strategies of textual seductiveness, see Ross Chambers, *Story and Situation: Narrative Seduction and the Power of Fiction* (Minneapolis: University of Minnesota Press, 1984).

23 See Tanner, *Adultery in the Novel*, 207.

24 Sartre, *L'Idiot de la famille*, II, 1284: "la vie apparaît à Flaubert comme un cycle de répétitions involutives: tout recommence toujours mais en se dégradant sans cesse. Ainsi appliquerait-il volontiers aux événements d'une vie individuelle la remarque que fera Marx, un peu plus tard, touchant les grandes circonstances de l'Histoire: les faits se reproduisent; la première fois ils sont vrais et tragiques, la second burlesque: ... "

25 See Sartre, *L'Idiot* ... , II, 1276–82. The dehumanizing of the protagonists in this passage is seen by Sartre as a failure to present a correspondence between a microcosmic segment and a macrocosmic totality. "c'est la mort de l'illusion: il n'y a plus de personnages, juste des figurants manipulés par un cinéaste," 1285.

26 The couple's relation to the decor is clearly fetishistic. On the importance of fetishistic structures of substitution in *L'Education sentimentale* and in *Bouvard et Pécuchet* see Bernheimer, *Flaubert and Kafka*, 102–17. I discuss fetishism in *Madame Bovary* in the concluding pages of this chapter.

27 Clément/Cixous, *La Jeune née*, 155–69. Cixous speaks of a bi-sexuality which does not nullify differences, but animates and proliferates them. Reversals of sexual roles in this passage of *Madame Bovary* function in a radically different manner; they underscore the polarization of sexuality, according to a schema dominated by masculine desire.

28 In commenting on this passage, Bernheimer notes its symmetrical relation to the passage I quoted earlier in which Emma becomes the "loving woman of all novels, the heroine of all dramas ... " What Emma considers "real about the figure is precisely its function as a stimulus for metaphoric attribution." *Flaubert and Kafka*, 62.

29 See N. Schor, "Pour une thématique restreinte," 43–4.

30 See Charles Bernheimer's excellent study, *Flaubert and Kafka*, which contains interesting discussions of fetishistic structures in *L'Education sentimentale* and *Bouvard et Pécuchet*. Bernheimer distinguishes between two types of fetishes. The first is analogous to Emma's attachment to the cigar case discussed above in this chapter; examples are Frédéric's attraction to Madame Arnoux's shoes, the hem of her dress and the fur trim of her velvet coat. The second type of fetish is linguistic: "they are the codes of social discourse, discourse systematized into self-contained ideological structures. ... What precisely do the clerks fetishize? They replace the code of clichés that initially served to cement their relationship ... with a succession of books. Each of these books contains a specialized vocabulary, a hermeneutic code, that they adopt and cathect with Erotic energy," 109–10.

31 S. Freud, "Fetishism," transl. J. Strachey, *Second Edition*, XXI (London: Hogarth Press, 1961), 149–57.

32 J. Derrida, *Glas* (Paris: Galilée, 1974), 252–4: "La consistence, la résistance, la restance du fétiche est à la mesure de son lien indécidable à des contraires. Le fétiche – en général – ne commence donc à exister

141

qu'en tant qu'il commence à se lier à des contraires. Ce double lien, ce double ligament définit donc sa structure la plus subtile". 253.

4. The autobiography of rhetoric: on reading Rimbaud's *Une Saison en enfer*

1 Quotations from *Une Saison en enfer* are taken from the Susanne Bernard edition of Arthur Rimbaud's *Oeuvres* (Paris: Garnier, 1960).

2 One of the most interesting aspects of this text is its resistance to definition. It repeats nostalgically many Romantic themes in the discovery of their bankruptcy; the "absolute" modernism at the end of the poem eludes, precisely, the finality which the narrator claims to seek. The poem is perhaps most modern in revealing the limits of interpretive categories, either those which are articulated within the text, or those which the critic might bring ready-made to his or her reading.

3 My use of the terms *histoire* and *discours* is derived from E. Benveniste's well-known studies on subjectivity in language, the system of verb tenses in French, and of shifters. See E. Benveniste, "L'Homme dans le langage," in *Problèmes de linguistique générale* (Paris: Gallimard, 1966), 225–88; Gérard Genette, *Figures III* (Paris: Seuil, 1972), esp. 71–8, 225–43, 261–5.

4 Paul de Man, "Excuses" in *Allegories of Reading*. (New Haven and London: Yale University Press), 279.

5 Laurent Jenny, "Il n'y a pas de récit cathartique," *Poétique*, 41 (février 1980), 1–21, discusses a similar disjunction between the narrating and narrated subject in his study of narrative in Breuer's and Freud's writings on hysteria. "Comment parvenir à *pratiquer* par le récit cette division instantanée et insaisissable qui fait que, dans toute proféération du *Je*, je m'éloigne de moi-même, à peine me suis-je posé?" 16.

6 J. L. Austin, *How To Do Things with Words*, ed. J. O. Urmson, Marins Sbisà (Cambridge, Mass.: Harvard University Press, 1975), 8.

7 J. Derrida, "La Double Séance," in *La Dissémination* (Paris: Seuil, 1972), 219–22. See Ross Chambers, "Récits d'aliénés, récits aliénés," *Poétique*, 53 (février 1983) 72–80.

8 For a discussion of the structural functions of actants in *Une Saison en enfer*, see A.-M. Lilti, "Essai d'analyse structurale d'*Une Saison en enfer*," *Languages*, 31 (1973), 112–26, esp. 116.

9 No narrative which uses the first person pronoun can be called *histoire* in Benveniste's sense of the term; what interests me here are the degrees of discursivity which can be elucidated in the differences between the narrated past and the present of narration. Starobinski notes that traits which characterize *discours* frequently become "contaminated" by those which are common to *histoire*; the first person may be treated like a third person in a text which adopts the tenses of *histoire*. Jean Starobinski, "Le Style de l'autobiographe," *Poétique*, 3

(1970), 257–65. (See 262.) In Rimbaud's text, the "contamination" works in radically different ways.

10 See S. Leclaire, *Psychanalyser* (Paris: Seuil, 1968), 181–6, "De même que le phallus peut être dit simultanément lettre de la lettre et objet type, de même *la castration* peut être définie comme le *modèle de toute articulation possible* pour autant qu'elle constitue l'accès immédiat à la faille en même temps qu'à son franchissement. Car le rapport du phallus à l'ensemble des lettres – ce qu'est la castration – fait immédiatement apparaître *ce en quoi consiste une articulation: un rapport au zero, un agencement qui permet une relation avec le manque*" (185).

11 *Deny* is used here in the sense generally attributed to Freud's term: *Verneinung*, the negation which both denies and affirms.

12 See M. Foucault, *Les Mots et les Choses* (Paris: Gallimard, 1966), 9–10, and especially, 323–9.

13 Paul de Man, "Semiology and Rhetoric," in *Allegories of Reading*, 3–19, esp. 9–10.

14 On the function of the term *farce* in Marx's writings on Louis Bonaparte to indicate the disruption of history and the failure of representation, see my last chapter.

15 Shoshana Felman, "Arthur Rimbaud; folie et modernité," in *La Folie et la chose littéraire* (Paris: Seuil, 1978), comments on the interplay between *délire/dé-lire*, between delirium and a "generalized deconstruction of classical reading" in *Une Saison en enfer*, 108–11, esp. 108–9.

16 *La Folie et la chose littéraire*, 114.

17 My last chapter, in an analysis of Flaubert's and Baudelaire's trials for obscenity, discusses the wider ideological and political implications of destabilizing patriarchal models of sexuality.

18 I use Lacan's term *Imaginaire* in the same sense defined by Jean Laplanche and J.-P. Pontalis in *Vocabulaire de la psychanalyse* (Paris: P.U.F., 1973), 195–6. The imaginary is one of the three essential registers of the psychoanalytic field, which includes the real, the symbolic and the imaginary. "La notion d'"imaginaire' se comprend d'abord en référence à une des premières élaborations théoriques de Lacan concernant le *stade du miroir*. Dans le travail qu'il a consacré à celui-ci l'auteur mettait en évidence l'idée que le moi du petit humain, du fait en particulier de la prématuration biologique, se constitue à partir de l'image de son semblable (moi spéculaire)."

19 *La Folie et la chose littéraire*, 112. "Le discours de la rupture n'est jamais absolument moderne. Le désir de la modernité originaire et non répétitive est lui-même voué à la forme et au paradoxe de la répétition."

5. False confusions: fictions of masculine desire in Mallarmé's "L'Après-midi d'un faune"

1 All references to Mallarmé are to Stéphane Mallarmé, *Oeuvres*

Complètes, ed. Henri Mondor, C. Jean-Aubry (Paris: Gallimard, "Pléiade," 1945).

2 Writing to Théodore Aubanel in summer 1865, Mallarmé discusses an early version of the poem, entitled "Monologue d'un faune," 1450.

3 Leo Bersani's excellent study of Mallarmé, *The Death of Stéphane Mallarmé* (London and New York: Cambridge University Press, 1982) discusses the "critical imperialism" of exegetical readings of Mallarmé and proposes a criticism which would "emphasize the radical unlocatability of meaning in literary language ... Criticism, far from solving the enigmas of literature, has perhaps even put into question the very category of the enigma by dissolving it in a more radical view of literary language (a view to which narrative resolutions of enigmatic sense are irrelevant) as continuously performing the deferral, or the absence, of its meanings" p. viii.

4 See, for example, Jean-Pierre Richard, *L'Univers imaginaire de Mallarmé* (Paris: Seuil, 1961), 295–7. Malcolm Bowie in his chapter on "Difficulty," *Mallarmé and the Art of Being Difficult* (Cambridge, England: Cambridge University Press, 1978), 3–18, notes the two opposing tendencies of Mallarmé criticism, which either accord privilege to descriptive elements at the expense of attention to abstractions, or concentrate on interpreting the texts as abstract, metaphysical voyages. The suggestive richness of the texts, however, comes from the interplay between the abstract and the material continuities.

5 Maurice Blanchot, "Le Mythe de Mallarmé" in *La Part du feu* (Paris: Gallimard, 1949), 35–48.

6 Jacques Derrida, "La Double séance," *La Dissémination* (Paris: Seuil, 1972) "La supplémentarité n'est pas ici, comme en apparence ou en conscience chez Rousseau, le mouvement unilatéral qui, tombant au dehors, perd dans l'espace et la vie et la chaleur d'une parole; c'est l'excès d'un signifiant qui, en son dedans, supplée l'espace et répète l'ouverture. Le livre alors n'est plus la réparation mais la répétition de l'espacement, de ce qui s'y joue, s'y perd, s'y gagne.... Loin de remplacer la scène ou de substituer une intériorité maitrisée à l'échappée d'un espace cette suppléance retient et répète implacablement la scène dans le livre," 265.

7 Blanchot, "Le Mythe de Mallarmé," 37–8.

8 See Luce Irigaray, *Speculum de l'autre Femme* (Paris: Minuit, 1974), 9–162, for a discussion of Freud's writings on femininity and what is at stake in maintaining oppositions such as masculine/feminine, active/passive.

9 See Sam Weber's discussion on the importance of narrative in "infantile sexual theories" in Freud's discussions of the "castration complex." "Observation, Description, Figurative Language," *The Legend of Freud* (Minneapolis: University of Minnesota Press, 1982), 17–31. "The development of desire, as Freud describes it in *The Interpretation of Dreams*, is tied not to the perception of objects, but to their

hallucination. The decisive modification implied by the 'castration complex' is that the deployment of desire implies not merely the production of hallucinations, but their organization into a story. The story of castration attempts to temporize the contradiction between "perception" and "prejudice" by temporalizing it . . ." 23–4.

10 See Roland Barthes, "L'Effet de réel," *Communications*, 11 (1968), 84–9.
11 My discussion of description draws upon Philippe Hamon's theory of description, particularly "Descriptif et Savoir" in *Introduction à l'analyse du Descriptif* (Paris, Hachette, 1981), 31–3, and notes 12, 83.
12 See Hamon, *Introduction à l'analyse du Descriptif*, 53.
13 Blanchot, "Le Mythe de Mallarmé," 46.
14 Readers have interpreted the instability of the scene in "L'Après-midi . . ." as evidence that Mallarmé is projecting an artificial decor from the faun's vital consciousness. Jean-Pierre Richard notes: "il manifeste un vigoreux *dedans* et un *dehors* qui n'a plus d'existence. Il ne lui reste plus alors qu'à créer un nouveau *dehors*, un dehors faux, mais susceptible cependant d'acceuillir d'une certaine manière en lui l'expansion intime." *L'Univers imaginaire de Mallarmé*, 295. In Richard's analysis, the poem would be about the preference for the imaginary over the real, and certainly the traces of the Narcissus myth might sustain this reading. This may be the tradition upon which Mallarmé's text draws, yet, in its repetitions of the old story, the poem distorts it in reflections which can never be reconstructed. Rather than projecting upon the artificial a lost meaning, mythical or personal and lyrical, the poem is about divisions and differences whose dynamics never allow the retrieval of an original simple presence or the projections of a reflected double.
15 On puns in this poem, see Roseline Crawley, "Toward the Poetics of Juxtaposition: 'L'Après-midi d'un faune'," *Yale French Studies*, 54 (197), 33–44.
16 Roger Dragonetti, "Métaphysique et poétique dans l'oeuvre de Mallarmé ('Hérodiade," 'Igitur,' 'Le Coup de dès')" *Revue de Métaphysique et de Morale*, 84, (1979), 366–93.
17 Blanchot, "Le mythe de Mallarmé," 44.
18 I refer here to the well-known passage in "La musique et les lettres": "Orage, lustral; et, dans des bouleversements, tout à l'acquit de la génération, récente, l'acte d'écrire se scruta jusqu'en l'origine. Très avant, au moins, quant au point, je le formule: – A savoir s'il y a lieu d'écrire," 645.
19 "La Musique et les lettres," 649.
20 "Préface," "Un Coup de dès," 455.
21 "Mais la fonction du titre n'est pas seulement de hiérarchie. Le titre à suspendre est aussi, par sa place, suspendu, en suspens ou en suspension. Au-dessus d'un texte dont il attend et reçoit tout – ou rien. Entre autres gôles, cette suspension se tient donc au lieu où Mallarmé a

disposé le *lustre*, les innombrables lustres sur la scène des textes."
Derrida, "La Double séance," 205.

22 Paul de Man, *Allegories of Reading* (New Haven and London: Yale
University Press, 1979), 18.

23 Emile Benveniste, "La Nature des pronoms," *Problèmes de Linguistique Générale* (Paris: Gallimard, 1966), 251–7.

24 Leo Bersani, "The Man Dies," *The Death of Stéphane Mallarmé*, 1–24.

25 I use the term Imaginary in Lacan's sense to refer to the alienating
identification which takes place in the so-called "mirror stage" of
development, and which is accompanied by "libidinal dynamism" and
aggressivity: "Il suffit de comprendre le stade du miroir comme une
identification au sens plein que l'analyse donne à ce terme: à savoir la
transformation produite chez le sujet, quant il assume une image, –
dont la prédestination à cet effet de phase est suffisamment indiquée
par l'usage, dans la théorie, du terme antique d'imago ... le point
important est que cette forme situe l'instance du *moi*, dès avant sa
détermination sociale, dans une ligne de fiction, à jamais irréductible
pour le seul individu, – ou plutôt, qui ne rejoindra qu'asymptoti-
quement le devenir du sujet, quel que soit le succès des synthèses
dialectiques par quoi il doit résoudre en tant que *je* sa discordance
d'avec sa propre réalité." "Le Stade du miroir," *Ecrits* (Paris: Seuil,
1966), 94.

6. The trials of authority under Louis Bonaparte

1 I use the term hegemony in the sense outlined by Gramsci to define the
network of cultural and political relationships through which a dominant group exercises its authority. Power is not imposed directly, but is
sustained by implicit consent from the governed. The functions of
hegemony are "organizational and connective," and comprise (1) "the
'spontaneous' consent given by the great masses of the population to
the general direction imposed on social life by the dominant fundamental group ... " and (2) the apparatus of state coercive power, which
"legally" enforces discipline on those groups which do not "consent,"
either actively or passively. See: "The Intellectuals," in *The Prison
Notebooks: Selections*, translated and edited by Quentin Hoare and
Geoffrey Nowell Smith (New York: International Publishers, 1971),
12. See also "The Modern Prince": "Undoubtedly the fact of hegemony presupposes the fact that account be taken of the interests and the
tendencies of the groups over which hegemony is to be exercised, and
that a certain compromise equilibrium should be formed ... " 161.

2 Karl Marx, *The Class Struggles in France: 1848–1850*. Introduction by
Frederick Engels (New York: International Publishers, 1972); *The 18th
Brumaire of Louis Bonaparte*, in Karl Marx, Frederick Engels, *Collected Works*, vol. I: 1851–53 (New York: International Publishers,
1979).

3 Fredric Jameson, "On Interpretation," in *The Political Unconscious, Narrative as a Socially Symbolic Act* (Ithaca: Cornell University Press, 1981), 17–102, uses this expression to refer to histories which seek a master narrative which relies upon the twin categories of the expressive subject and narrative closure (*telos*), 29.

4 Louis Althusser, "Idéologie et appareils idéologiques d'état" in *Positions* (Paris: Editions sociales, 1976), 67–125. Art, along with other cultural institutions, serves the authority of the state, according to Althusser, not because it is coercive or repressive but because its own configurations intertwine with those of the political/economic sphere. Althusser's well-known analysis of the circulation of power distinguishes between the state apparatus, the government, administration, army, police, courts, prisons, etc., and the ideological apparatus of the state, the church, the schools, the family, courts (which belong to both spheres), the political parties, the press and the arts, by which hegemony is maintained (86). Ideology is the "imaginary representation of individuals to their real conditions of existence," (101) which depends upon a system of mis-representations and is exercised through certain rituals (107), with the central category being that of the subject (110).

5 See J.-P. Sartre, *Baudelaire* (Paris: Gallimard, 1947); *L'Idiot de la famille* (Paris: Gallimard, vols. I and II, 1971; vol. III, 1972). See also Douglas Collins, *Sartre as Biographer* (Cambridge, Mass. and London, England: Harvard University Press, 1980). I do not wish to rehearse once again the problems of how each of these writers accommodates himself to the social and affective alienation of the artist in mid and late nineteenth-century France; while railing against the pervasive mediocrity of the times, each accepted certain accommodations with an expanding, triumphant bourgeois culture, including even the (colonialist) adventurer, Rimbaud. Their writings, nonetheless, powerfully disrupt the imaginary representations which sustain bourgeois power. Sartre's work on Flaubert and Baudelaire, as is well known, takes their moral complicity with bourgeois culture as its starting point.

6 F. Jameson, in *The Political Unconscious*, has distinguished three levels of interpretation for analyzing the articulations between the literary text and the wider social text. At the first level, the individual work is studied as a more or less discrete symbolic system. On a second level, the individual text can be linked with the broader social order: the object of study here is the *ideologeme*: "the smallest intelligible unit of the essentially antagonistic collective discourses of social classes." The final perspective is that of "history as a whole," an analysis of what Jameson calls the ideology of form: "the symbolic messages transmitted to us by the co-existence of various sign systems," 76. While I do not aim at the ultimately totalizing interpretive finality underlying Jameson's project, which would impose a Marxist master-narrative inimical to the inquiry carried out in this book, what follows can be articulated in general sense with the symbolic processes of the second and third levels

of analysis. See also R. Terdiman's interesting discussion of the "conflict of discourse" in mid nineteenth-century France in *Discourse / Counter-Discourse* (forthcoming, Cornell University Press), especially his theoretical introduction.

7 Marx, *The 18th Brumaire*, 103.
8 Marx, *The 18th Brumaire*, 103–4.
9 Marx, *The 18th Brumaire*, 106.
10 Foucault has discussed this double movement of displaced origin in nineteenth-century thought; origin which has retreated out of grasp into an irretrievable past is sought in projections upon the future: "en se donnant pour tache de restituer le domaine de l'originaire, la pensée moderne y découvre aussitôt le recul de l'origine; et elle se propose paradoxalement d'avancer dans la direction où ce recul s'accomplit et ne cesse de s'approfondir; elle essaie de le faire apparâître de l'autre côté de l'expérience, comme ce qui la soutient par son retrait même, comme ce qui est au plus proche de sa possibilité la plus visible, comme ce qui est, en elle, imminent. ..." Michel Foucault, *Les Mots et les Choses* (Paris: Gallimard, 1966), 344–5.
11 Sartre, *L'Idiot*, III, 532. See also Collins, 166. The terms farce, parody, joke, travesty, masquerade, appear throughout *The 18th Brumaire* and *Class Struggles in France*. "[Louis Bonaparte was] clumsily cunning, knavishly naive, doltishly sublime, a calculated superstition, a pathetic burlesque, a cleverly stupid anachronism, a world historical piece of buffoonery and an undeciphered hieroglyph for the understanding of the civilized ..." *Class Struggles*, 71.
12 Jeffrey Mehlman, *Revolution and Repetition: Marx/Hugo/Balzac* (Berkeley, Los Angeles, London: University of California Press, "Quantum," 1977), 5–41.
13 By mis-representation, I refer to the problem discussed by Althusser concerning distortions which individuals assume to be the "natural order" of things in the representations of their relations as "subject" to the discourse of power. When ideology forms subjects, it imposes as transparent and self-evident symbolic operations which subject the individual to a specific discourse of power: misrepresentation is the condition of representation. See "Appareils idéologiques d'état," 111.
14 Mehlman, 20–1.
15 Mehlman, 14; Marx, *Class Struggles*, 68; *The 18th Brumaire*, 187–8.
16 Marx, *Class Struggles*, 71–2.
17 Marx, *Class Struggles*, 109.
18 Marx, *Class Struggles*, 111.
19 Marx, *Class Struggles*, 112.
20 It will be seen below in a discussion of the two trials for obscenity, that the judicial system had a considerable stake in guarding against just such slippages in the symbolic system. The literary text must be held accountable for the stable sense of its language. A certain heteronomy

thus prepares the way for that heteronomy which Marx decries later in *The 18th Brumaire* (185).
21 Marx, *The 18th Brumaire*, 114.
22 Marx, *Class Struggles*, 67.
23 Marx, *Class Struggles*, 71.
24 Marx, *Class Struggles*, 71.
25 Marx, *The 18th Brumaire*, 187–9.
26 Marx, *The 18th Brumaire*, 194.
27 Marx, *The 18th Brumaire*, 195.
28 Marx, *The 18th Brumaire*, 193.
29 Marx, *The 18th Brumaire*, 194. Françoise Gaillard, in her essay "A Little Story about the *bras de fer*; or, How History is made," has noted the crucial importance of linguistic imperialism in the unsettled times following the revolution and its formative role in flaubertian *bêtise*. The undeniable successes of stupidity "are due less to the persuasive power of stupidity's speech than to its linguistic imperialism: because of its inability to promote successfully a universalizable interest that, at the level of content, would bring about a consensus, *la bêtise* replaces it by a universalist language ethic. After the revolutionary shake-up which left each person separated and enclosed in his fear, French society can recompose itself only on the level of language, reunify itself only with the aid of a common language, and *la bêtise* is this koine, ... " 98. "A Little Story about the *bras de fer*," in *Flaubert and Post-modernism*, ed. Naomi Schor, Henry Majewski (Lincoln, Neb., and London, England: University of Nebraska Press, 1984), 84–97.
30 Mehlman, 14–15.
31 Marx, *The 18th Brumaire*, 194.
32 Jameson, 47.
33 Marx, *The 18th Brumaire*: "The cause [the interests of the middle class] must accordingly be kept alive; but the effect where it manifests itself, must be done away with. But this cannot pass off without slight confusions of cause and effect, since in their interaction both lose their distinguishing features," 194.
34 For the dossier of Baudelaire's trial, see Charles Baudelaire, *Les Fleurs du mal*, in *Oeuvres complètes*, ed. Jacques Crépet (Paris: Conard, 1930); the documents of Flaubert's trial are reprinted in *Madame Bovary*, ed. E. Maynial (Paris: Garnier, 1961). Referred to hereafter as: "Baudelaire: Trial," and "Flaubert: Trial."
35 Dominick La Capra, *Madame Bovary on Trial* (Ithaca and London: Cornell University Press, 1982). In what follows, I will briefly summarize La Capra's reading of the trial in the first two chapters of his book; my own observations on the text of the trial will link La Capra's analysis more closely with the general problematic which I am discussing here.
36 See Edward Said, *Beginnings: Intention and Method* (Baltimore and London: The Johns Hopkins University Press, 1975) for an excellent discussion of the terms authority and author and the imbrication

between meanings which indicate the power to originate and others which, concurrently, refer to the power to control: "Taken together these meanings are all grounded in the following notions: 1) that of the power of an individual to initiate, institute, establish – in short, to begin; 2) that this power and its product are an increase over what had been there previously; 3) that the individual wielding this power controls its issue and what is derived therefrom; 4) that authority maintains the continuity of its course," 83. See also Jacques Derrida, "L'Otobiographie de Nietzsche," in *L'Oreille de l'Autre: Textes et Débats avec Jacques Derrida*, ed. Claude Lévesque, Christie V. Mc-Donald (Montréal: v1b éditeur, 1982), 13–56, on the politics of the proper name.

37 La Capra, 30–3.
38 La Capra, 44; Flaubert: Trial, 351.
39 See J. L. Austin, *How To Do Things with Words* (Cambridge, Mass.: Harvard University Press, 1975) for a discussion of performatives, those utterances which perform an action, such as contractual and declarative statements. See also Mary Louise Pratt, *Toward a Speech Act Theory of Literary Discourse* (Bloomington and London: Indiana University Press, 1977).
40 Foucault, *L'Ordre du discours* (Paris: Gallimard, 1971), 12. This subversive potential of discourse is one of its most powerful aspects, as Foucault has noted: "le discours n'est pas simplement ce qui traduit les luttes ou les systèmes de domination, mais ce pour quoi, ce par quoi on lutte, le pouvoir dont on cherche à s'emparer."
41 Flaubert: Trial, 345.
42 La Capra, 39.
43 La Capra, 43
44 La Capra, 43.
45 Baudelaire: Trial, 331.
46 Baudelaire: Trial, 337.
47 Baudelaire: Trial, 333.
48 Baudelaire: Trial, 331.
49 Foucault, in *L'Ordre du discours*, has noted that the power of discourse is intimately linked to its ability to define through exclusion. Censorship, it might be added, is but a limited manifestation of this power to exclude: "Dans une société comme la nôtre, on connaît, bien sûr, les procédures d'exclusion. La plus évidente, la plus familière aussi, c'est l'interdit. On sait bien qu'on n'a pas le droit de tout dire, qu'on ne peut pas parler de tout dans n'importe quelle circonstance, que n'importe qui, enfin, ne peut pas parler de n'importe quoi. Tabou de l'objet, rituel de la circonstance, droit privilégié ou exclusif du sujet qui parle . . . " 11.
50 See Emile Benveniste, "La Nature des pronoms," *Problèmes de linguistique générale* (Paris: Gallimard, 1966), 251–66.
51 Baudelaire: Trial, 334.
52 Baudelaire: Trial, 334.

53 See Jacques Derrida, *La Dissémination* (Paris: Seuil, 1972).

54 Baudelaire: Trial, 323. In the summary arguments, this threat is again referred to as a sickness: "cette fièvre malsaine qui porte à tout peindre, à tout décrire, à tout dire . . ." 336.

55 It is possible to read the defense's awkward prose as evoking the figure of the mythic hermaphrodite, a figure of sexual completeness, which precedes division into separate male and female bodies. Divided and errant sexuality is too prevalent and too anxious a concern in the commentaries of both the prosecution and defense to admit that possibility. See C. Clément, H. Cixous, *La Jeune née* (Paris: Union générale d'éditions, 10/18, 1975). In her discussion of bisexuality, Cixous characterizes the hermaphrodite of Ovid in these terms: "La bisexualité comme fantasme d'un être total qui vient à la place de la peur de la castration, et voile la différence sexuelle dans la mesure où celle-ci est éprouvée comme marque d'une sécabilité dangereuse et douloureuse. C'est l'Hermaphrodite, d'Ovide, moins bisexué qu'asexueé, composé non pas des deux genres, mais de deux moitiés. Fantasme donc d'unité. Deux en un, et encore même pas deux," 155.

56 Baudelaire: Trial, 338.

57 Baudelaire: Trial, 339.

58 See Terdiman, "The Paradoxes of Distinction: The Prose Poem as Prose," in *Discourse / Counter-discourse*, for the wider significance of the hegemonic force of prose as the dominant discourse of the mid nineteenth century.

59 Baudelaire: Trial, 339.

60 Baudelaire: Trial, 341.

61 Baudelaire: Trial, 340.

62 Baudelaire: Trial, 334.

63 J.-J. Goux, in *Les Faux Monnayeurs du Langage* (Paris: Galilée, 1984), has discussed the importance of the monetary metaphor, which is called upon to validate a view of the poet as prince in the mid-nineteenth century, capable of assuming complete authority for his voice. What is said here about Victor Hugo would be consistent with the defense's position on Baudelaire: "Ainsi, pour Victor Hugo, l'écrivain est semblable à un prince. Il bat monnaie. Il imprime sa marque à l'avers de la langue. 'Tout grand écrivain frappe la prose à son éffigie' énonce Hugo. Ou mieux encore: 'Les poètes sont comme les souverains. Ils doivent battre monnaie. Il faut que leur éffigie reste sur les idées qu'ils mettent en circulation.' L'écrivain, s'il est grand, laisse sa marque propre par l'originalité de son style, la frappe d'une impression qui donne une nouvelle figure aux signes de la langue. Il n'est pas seulement auteur, mais autorité émmetrice. Il est vraiment auctoritas." 133–4.

64 Naomi Schor, "In the Academy, or Gendering Details," a chapter of a forthcoming book on the detail, notes that in the neo-Classical esthetic tradition the detail constitutes a threat to the hierarchic ordering of the

work of art: "The irreconcilability of details and the sublime and the concomitant affinity of details for the effete and effeminate ornamental style point to what is perhaps most threatening about the detail: its tendency to subvert an internal hierarchic ordering of the work of art which clearly subordinates the periphery to the center, the accessory to the principal, the foreground to the background," 13. Schor also quotes a passage from Baudelaire's essay on Constantin Guys, "Le Peintre de la vie moderne," in which the detail is associated with the disruption of a "just" esthetic equilibrium and metaphorized as an anarchic revolutionary mob: "Un artiste ayant le sentiment parfait de la forme, mais accoutumé à exercer surtout sa mémoire et son imagination, se trouve alors comme assailli par une émeute de détails, qui tous demandent justice avec la furie d'une foule amoureuse d'égalité absolue. Toute justice se trouve forcément violée; toute harmonie détruite, sacrifiée; mainte trivialité devient énorme; mainte petitesse, usurpatrice. Plus l'artiste se penche avec impartialité vers le détail, plus l'anarchie augmente. Qu'il soit myope ou presbyte, toute hiérarchie et toute subordination disparaissent." Baudelaire, *Oeuvres complètes* (Paris: Gallimard, "Pléiade," 1961), 1167.

65 Baudelaire, in the notes submitted to his lawyer, strongly emphasized the architectural coherence of his volume. See: "Notes et documents pour mon avocat," in *Les Fleurs du mal*, 326–8.

66 There is only one example cited to counter the charge that *Les Fleurs du mal* are offensive to religious morality, a poem by Lamartine. The anguished complaint quoted from "Désespoir," in Lamartine's "Harmonies poétiques," is cited as blasphemous, yet it remains securely in its place within an equilibrium between devotion and despair, fully accountable for in the context of Christian morality and esthetics.

67 Baudelaire: Trial, 351.

68 Baudelaire: Trial, 352–3.

69 Baudelaire: Trial, 355.

70 Baudelaire: Trial, 355. J. Derrida, "La Double Séance," in *La Dissémination* (Paris: Seuil, 1972), has analyzed the logic of mimesis in Plato, particularly the interrelation between the model and its derived representation: see especially, 211–12.

INDEX